A poignant memoir. Each story [...]
layer at a time until I felt as if Ra[...]
the kitchen with me as I sautée[...]
humility, and spot-on prose, I came away with a deeper appreciation for the ties that bind, for the complexities of mother-daughter
relationships, and for the healing power of food at the family table.
This book does as much to feed the spirit as it does the body, and I'm
betting readers will be begging for seconds.

> **Julie Cantrell,** *New York Times* and *USA Today*
> bestselling author of *Into the Free*

As engaging as a novel. A delicious book.

> **Dianna Booher,** author of *Communicate with Confidence*
> and *Creating Personal Presence*

Someone once said, "She who bakes bread without love nourishes
only half the man." I have eaten at Becky's table many times with
her husband, Greg, and I can tell you firsthand that when she serves
something from her kitchen, it nourishes the whole of you. For her
and her daughter, Rachel, food is a sacrament for the communion of
saints gathered around their table. So are laughter and tears. Come
hungry to this book's table of contents. When you're finished, you'll
come away full!

> **Ken Gire,** author of *Moments with the Savior*,
> *Windows of the Soul*, and *Relentless*

Unique. Special. Surprising. Entertaining. Humorous and heart-
warming. You will be rolling on the floor laughing one minute and
wiping a tear the next, while simultaneously whipping up a creative
recipe for your family.

> **Carol Kent,** speaker and author of *Between a Rock and a Grace Place*

Food is increasingly dividing us. How we need Becky and her daughter, Rachel, a vegan and a butter-loving mama to show us how to not
only break bread together, but to make bread — and soups and all
kinds of creative meals — together. This book is sure to inspire us
all (with fun and pizzazz) toward the communion and healing God
intended through food.

> **Leslie Leyland Fields,** author/edito[...]
> of *The Spirit of Food: 34 Writers on F[...]*

Surely one of life's greatest pleasures has to be gathering around a table of delicious food to share our favorite stories with family and friends. In *We Laugh, We Cry, We Cook* this mother-daughter duo gifts us with an abundance of both!

Shellie Rushing Tomlinson, Belle of All Things Southern and author of *Sue Ellen's Girl Ain't Fat, She Just Weighs Heavy!*

From the moment I received *We Laugh, We Cry, We Cook*, it was constantly in one hand while the other tended to kid-tastrophies. Rachel and Becky created a tasty memoir full of authenticity in the trenches of motherhood. If feeding a family is love—this is one book that will nurture any mother's heart and soul!

Heather Riggleman, speaker to MOPS moms and author of *Mama Needs a Time Out*

A delicious, well-marinated read! Mother-daughter stories that will touch your heart and then send you to the kitchen to try down-to-earth, tried-and-true recipes. I love this book!

Sue Buchanan, author of *The Bigger the Hair the Closer to God*

Mom Becky and daughter Rachel are as different as two people can be, but it's those differences that make this book delicious. If they were kitchen utensils, Rachel would be a bento box and Becky a salad spinner. Not just funny, these women are real. Tucked between recipes are the vulnerabilities, passions, regrets, and joys that make up family life. A yummy read!

Lucille Zimmerman, licensed professional counselor and author of *Renewed: Finding Your Inner Happy in an Overwhelmed World*

A heartwarming celebration of food, family, friendship, and fellowship. Warming and wise.

Patricia Raybon, author of *I Told the Mountain to Move*

Mothers and Daughters: if you can read only one book this year—this is it. *We Laugh, We Cry, We Cook* is a peephole into the lives and kitchens of a mother and daughter who are determined not to take themselves or each other too seriously. The results? More laughter, less friction. Spoiler alert: that's the best recipe in the book.

Rachel St. John-Gilbert, author of *The Well-Lived Laugh*

With a writing style as warm and delectable as the recipes and stories within *We Laugh, We Cry, We Cook*, this narrative is about a mother and daughter, their lives, and the kitchens they come from. This must-read book will inspire and entertain you!

Cheri Fuller, speaker and author of *Mother-Daughter Duet*
and *What a Son Needs From His Mom*

Becky and Rachel encourage us to take time to connect, listen, be fully present. To show us how the kitchen is once again, as it always has been, a glorious place to connect, belong, and feel seen and heard.

Tammy Maltby, Emmy award–winning TV cohost and
author of *The God Who Sees You* and *The Christmas Kitchen*

I adore this delightful mother-daughter take on the passionate elements of living: food, family, and finding ourselves ... and fun. Two thumbs up for this relational-foodie book that will keep you smiling, salivating, and scribbling grocery lists throughout every chapter.

Debora M. Coty, award-winning author
of *Fear, Faith, and a Fistful of Chocolate*

Food ... so important to the great stories of Jesus and true hospitality. I've been in Becky's home and enjoyed about a hundred great meals. This book with her daughter, Rachel, showcases the best of life around the table.

Hugh Halter, pastor and author of *The Tangible Kingdom*

With poignant stories Becky Johnson and Rachel Randolph show the beauty of a mother-daughter relationship no matter the differences, and how feeding others is an act of creativity, love, and a generational legacy. An inspiring, delightful book.

Lindsey O'Connor, journalist and author of *The Long Awakening*

Unlike Becky Johnson and Rachel Randolph, I am a writer who was *not* blessed with the *foodie* gene. So imagine my surprise to be drawn into the delicious blend of story and recipes, relationships and food, so skillfully assembled in these pages. It is such yummy heart-food that I couldn't *not* read it out loud to my daughter, who enjoyed every bite!

Margot Starbuck, author of *The Girl in the Orange Dress*
and *Permission Granted*

Much of life happens around the table: the company, connections, and conversations. *We Laugh, We Cry, We Cook* brings it all together with delicious recipes, engaging stories, and an extra helping of laughter. As a mom of daughters myself, I love the mom/daughter relationship that makes this book both a delight to read as well as a great resource for recipes.

Karol Ladd, author of *Positive Life Principles for Women*

You'll laugh, cry, sigh, and head to the kitchen while you read this book. With warmth, humor, and mutual admiration, Becky and Rachel share their cooking adventures, mother-daughter relationship, and deep faith in God's approving presence. They prove anyone can cook, and even kitchen mishaps can turn delightful, if served with love.

Judith Couchman, author of *The Art of Faith* and a lifelong foodie

You'll love this book whether cooking is your passion or merely a necessity, as it is for me. Becky and Rachel's funny and heart-warming stories inspire me to "offer healing and blessing to others" by sharing their delicious-sounding recipes. Imagine that!

Joan C. Webb, life coach, speaker, and author of *The Relief of Imperfection*

A lighthearted look at the food we feed our families and the thoughts and feelings behind it.

Michelle LaRowe, 2004 International Nanny of the Year and author of *Working Mom's 411*

We Laugh, We Cry, We Cook takes me back to memories nearly forgotten, and urges me forward toward tables yet to be shared. If you're hungry for something rich and deeply satisfying, this is it.

Michele Cushatt, author, speaker, and butter-lovin' foodie

We Laugh We Cry We Cook

**A MOM *and* DAUGHTER DISH
ABOUT *the* FOOD *that* DELIGHTS THEM
and the LOVE *that* BINDS THEM**

*Becky Johnson
and Rachel Randolph*

ZONDERVAN

We Laugh, We Cry, We Cook

Copyright © 2013 by Becky Johnson and Rachel Randolph

This title is also available as a Zondervan ebook. Visit www.zondervan.com/ebooks.

This title is also available in a Zondervan audio edition. Visit www.zondervan.fm.

Requests for information should be addressed to:

Zondervan, *Grand Rapids, Michigan* 49530

Library of Congress Cataloging-in-Publication Data

Johnson, Becky Freeman, 1959 –
    We laugh, we cry, we cook : a mom and daughter dish about the food that
delights them, and the love that binds them / Becky Johnson and Rachel Randolph.
      pages cm
    Includes bibliographical references and index.
    ISBN 978-0-310-33083-7 (softcover)
    1. Johnson, Becky Freeman, 1959 – 2. Randolph, Rachel, 1983 – 3. Cooking,
American. 4. Mothers and daughters – United States – Biography. I. Randolph,
Rachel, 1983 – II. Title.
TX715.J619 2013
641.5973 – dc23   2013012513

Published in association with the literary agency of WordServe Literary Group, Ltd.,
Highlands Ranch, Colorado 80130 www.wordserveliterary.core

Cover design: Connie Gabbert Design + Illustration
Cover photography: shutterstock® / istockphoto®
Interior calligraphy: Connie Gabbert Design + Illustration
Interior design: Beth Shagene
Editorial: Carolyn McCready, Sarah Kuipers, Bob Hudson

Printed in the United States of America

13 14 15 16 17 18 /DCI/ 22 21 20 19 18 17 16 15 14 13 12 11 10 9 8 7 6 5 4 3 2 1

To my grandchildren,
who bring such joy to Nonny's kitchen,
and my husband, Greg;
"Life began again, the day you took my hand"
—Becky

To Jared,
for giving me courage to write,
and Jackson, for giving me a story to tell
—Rachel

Contents

~

Laughter is brightest where food is best.

Irish Proverb

~

Prologue from Mother and Daughter

Feeding the people I love is a hands-on way of loving them. When you nourish and sustain someone, essentially, you're saying that you want them to thrive, to be happy and healthy and able to live well.

Shauna Niequest

Our kitchens and the kitchens we came from seem to have a universal pull on us. Good food, deep love, and hearty laughter become the tastes of heaven for the hungry souls gathered 'round our tables.

Food is perhaps the most commonly used metaphor that God uses to tell us something meaningful and eternal. From forbidden fruit to manna, to loaves and fishes, to bread and wine ... we could follow the thread of God's Unfolding Story by going from food to food, drink to drink, meal to meal in passage after passage of the Bible.

Maybe that's why there are so many hidden layers of meaning when we stir a pot of Mama's chili or cut into a ripe red watermelon and find our minds transported to picnics in the hot, verdant summers of childhood. Cooking engages every sense: the taste of homemade peach ice cream, the smell of sweet corn, the sounds of steak sizzling on the grill, the hard, smooth feel of a good crisp apple in the hand, the arresting beauty of fresh garden veggies artfully arranged on the lopsided ceramic plate you made at age nine. Unlike anything else, food sears itself into our memories.

This is why, when we feed others, we nourish them in a myriad of surprising and memorable ways. You never know what gooey grilled-cheese sandwich or steaming bowl of basil-tomato soup will become a comforting memory forever sealed in the heart of someone you love. "I may write about the smell of asparagus, the color of polenta, or the taste of figs still warm from the sun," Paula Butturini writes, "but all of it is a personal shorthand for weighing love and hunger, health and nourishment, secrets and revelations, illness and survival, comfort and celebration, and perhaps most of all, the joy and gift of being alive."[1] Indeed. Food is all this and more.

Besides the fun of the food itself, cooks share a jovial companionship in the kitchen. Laughing, chatting, and cooking with one another, preparing a good meal for our family and friends, is one of the ways we, as mother and daughter, bond best. In spite of our quirks, somehow in the kitchen ... it works. And if it doesn't work, it's usually funny. Then it becomes a story. And the story becomes a memory, and that bonds us too. Then we write it down and share it with others, as we've tried to do in this book.

So ultimately, it is all good.

Welcome to our kitchens and to the food and stories and memories that bubble up from them. We're so glad for your company at the table.

~

Note: After this introduction, Rachel and Becky will indicate who is speaking with our names before each section.

Recipe Notation Glossary

You might be asking yourself, "What's the difference between *vegan* and *vegetarian*, and who is this *gluten* and why are we trying to free him?" Here's a quick glossary to help you understand the terms following the recipes in this book. Some recipes can be easily modified to be vegetarian, vegan, or gluten free. In those instances, we've followed the term with the substitutes or omissions to make that variation. We want to show how easy it is to adjust meals for yourself or guests with dietary preferences. Of course, if you have dairy milk, real butter, or chicken stock on hand and a vegan or vegetarian recipe calls for almond milk, margarine, or vegetable stock, you could certainly make those substitutes as well.

- *Vegetarian:* Recipes marked *vegetarian* do not have meat or fish products; they may include eggs or dairy.

- *Vegan:* Recipes marked *vegan* do not contain meat, fish, dairy, or eggs. By its nature, a recipe that is vegan is also vegetarian, so for clarity we've marked these recipes "vegan/ vegetarian."

- *Gluten free:* Recipes marked gluten free do not have any gluten (wheat, barley, or rye).

Note: Some products may vary from brand to brand, so please read labels carefully if you are cooking for someone with a special diet or allergy. Look for the allergy warnings at the end of ingredient labels. It typically says if it contains eggs, milk (dairy), wheat (gluten), or fish. You may have to read more carefully to see if it's cooked with meat (look for things like chicken stock or lard). Unless allergies or food preferences are severe, it's often okay if it says it "may contain" these ingredients. Check with your guests first, though, as some allergies are severe.

Chapter 1

Mother's Intuition

No one who cooks, cooks alone.
Even at her most solitary,
a cook in the kitchen is surrounded
by generations of cooks past.
Laurie Colwin

BECKY

We were in Phoenix on vacation. It was morning and I was asleep, dreaming. In my dream I saw my married daughter's face, glowing, and then I heard—audibly—the words *"She is pregnant."* I woke up with a start. It felt less like a dream than a proclamation of joy.

I emailed Rachel about my dream and then settled outside on the patio to enjoy a cup of coffee. What if she really were pregnant? How wonderful that would be! Rachel would get to experience all the joy of being a mom, just as I've enjoyed being her mother through the years. As I sipped my coffee, my mind drifted back to earlier times. I recalled when Rach was in the slow process of turning from a child into a teenager, when I first glimpsed what my daughter might be like as a woman ... and as a friend.

At thirteen my little girl walked into the bathroom in her T-shirt, jeans, and tennis shoes, her hair pulled up in a ponytail. Thirty minutes later, she walked out looking like a model from a teen magazine. Her strawberry-blond hair fell around her shoulders in ringlets, and her cute dress—with the figure to match—

immediately made her dad and brothers nervous. Ordinarily she was a quiet girl. In fact, we worried about her shyness. But puberty not only brought out her beauty, it also brought out newfound conversational skills and an extremely dry wit.

The thing that most surprised me about Rachel's blossoming self was how much she loved things done carefully and in order. She liked her room organized, she kept her schoolwork filed, and she arranged her clothes in the order she planned to wear them. Those who know me know that I have basically made a cottage-industry career out of flubbing up. I was what Rachel refers to as a "challenging parent," and at times my scatterbrained style would exasperate her to the point of near breakdown.

At that time, however, as I was becoming a writer and speaker who was forced to rely on her wits to get around the country, I wanted to show Rachel that her mother had learned new and impressive organizing skills. So when I was asked to speak in Nashville, I thought it was the perfect opportunity to both bond with and impress my dubious daughter. I asked her to come along.

When we landed in Nashville, I showed her the brochures of all the historic places we could visit in Music City. It took my young teen no time to decide on the outlet mall. That afternoon we must have shopped, walked, and talked for five hours ... two happy chicks. The sun began to set and the air grew nippy. Our stomachs began to growl, and our feet were begging for relief, so we headed for the rental car.

"Do you think the hotel will have a Jacuzzi?" Rachel asked as she struggled to make the last few feet to the car.

"I bet they do, babe," I replied as I fumbled through my purse for my keys. "We'll have to check it out, won't we? Hey, Rach, you don't have the keys, do you?"

"What?"

"I can't seem to find the car keys."

Her palm went immediately to her forehead, dramatically.

A gust of cold wind sent chills up our aching spines as we trudged back toward the mile-long train of stores. Forty-five minutes later, after retracing every step we'd taken, I found the precious keys in the corner of a dressing room, just moments before the mall closed for the night.

Exhausted and frozen, our stomachs now screaming for food, we fell into the car with twin sighs of relief.

"Mom," Rachel said, her voice trembling from fatigue and cold, "you're going to give me gray hair before I'm fourteen."

I smiled weakly and started the engine. As we drove away, I offered cheerfully, "I'll take you any place you want for dinner! I know a great little Italian bistro, or maybe you'd like to go to a fancy restaurant at Opryland?"

"Do they have any drive-through hamburger places in Nashville?" she asked.

So on our first big mom-daughter trip together, in a city filled with fancy eateries, we drove through Krystal Burgers and ordered six sliders with fries, enjoying every greasy bite. On the way to the hotel, we decided to make a quick stop at a local drugstore to pick up Crayolas and a couple of coloring books.

Once settled in our room, we took turns taking luxurious hot baths and washing our hair. We toweled up our tresses, turban style, then donned warm jammies, robes, and snuggly house slippers. I flipped on the TV, a special treat for us because we were one of those near-extinct families who did not own a television.

This particular night two Christmas specials were airing. The first was *Touched by an Angel*, and the other, a charming true story called *A Thousand Men and a Baby*. As we settled in to enjoy the programs, I spread out on the night stand between us some gourmet snacks I'd purchased at the outlet mall: sesame crackers, jalapeño jelly, and a spicy hummus dip.

Rachel and I whiled away the evening like two girls at a slumber party. We enjoyed the movies, munched happily on our goodies, and colored pictures like enthusiastic kindergarteners. I remember thinking, "These are the moments a mother lives for."

At one point I glanced up from my coloring book to see Rachel busy organizing her side of the room. Her clothes were folded and stacked in neat little squares and triangles, like party sandwiches. Her toiletries were arranged on the shelf in perfect ascending and descending order. Even her bedcovers were straight and smooth as she sat crossed-legged on them, smelling of citrus body lotion and fresh shampoo.

"Honey," I smiled, "your side of the room looks like it has been 'touched by an angel.'"

She glanced in my direction and raised an eyebrow. My bed was in crumpled disarray, and my suitcase stood open at one corner, spewing clothes across the bedspread. Cracker crumbs and bits of jalapeño jelly stuck to the front of my old nightshirt. I licked a bit of stray hummus from my finger and smiled.

"Mom," she said, "it looks like 'a thousand men and a baby' just had a party on your side of the room."

In spite of our differences, Rachel and I had a wonderful time, and our weekend drew to a close much too soon. As we stood in line at the Nashville airport to check our luggage and get our boarding passes, we recounted all the happy memories of our trip. Then a most unpleasant thing occurred. My suitcase exploded. Apparently the additional loot I'd purchased at the outlet mall had stretched the zipper beyond its abilities. It gave up the ghost with an audible rip, and the contents spilled onto the floor.

If you want to mortify a teenager, try sitting on the floor of a nice airport with your bras and underwear scattered all around you. Rach disappeared around the nearest support column as the ticket lady handed me a big roll of duct tape, which I wrapped around the suitcase, feeling like a character in one of Jeff Foxworthy's routines: "You know you're a redneck if you latch your Samsonite with duct tape!"

After my suitcase was taped and loaded onto the plane, I found Rachel several yards away, pretending not to know me. Thankfully the flight home went off without a hitch—at least until we landed at Dallas–Fort Worth airport when I realized I couldn't remember where I parked the car.

We spent the next couple of hours walking up and down endless rows of parked vehicles, hauling our luggage, including my embarrassing duct-taped suitcase. Finally, in desperation, we developed an emergency strategy. I would leave Rachel with the suitcases while I went on a search-and-rescue mission for our car. When I finally found it, I returned to find my tired daughter sitting atop the beleaguered luggage, looking like an orphan from some foreign war, soberly munching on a sugar cookie.

"Rach?" I asked, "where'd you get the cookie?"

"A lady walked by and said, 'Honey, you look like you could use a cookie.'" Rachel breathed a sign of exasperation as she put her head in her hands. "Mom, she thought I was homeless."

I told her the good news that I'd found the car—actually not far from her temporary post—which seemed to perk her up. We walked to the car with a renewed spring in our step, and after loading up the luggage, we climbed in. I looked over at Rachel and gave her hand a squeeze. She was on her last emotional leg, tears pooling at the corners of her eyes, so I gave her a quick little pep talk. "Rachel, I know this has been hard, but you and I—we're a team of women survivors! We're like Thelma and Louise! We're like Helen Keller and Annie Sullivan. We're like—"

"Mom," she interrupted me, brushing away a lone tear, "let's face it; we're like Dumb and Dumber."

I laughed and turned the key.

The car wouldn't start. The battery was dead.

By the time we found help, got the car started, and made it home, it was the wee hours of the morning.

A mere forty-eight hours or so later, Rachel actually began speaking to me again.

~

Then my mind flashed forward to Rachel's graduation from high school. Rachel looked so grown up and gorgeous, her curls piled up on her head in a Victorian upsweep. The event was held in the high school gym, and I was seated near the top of the bleachers. I'd brought along a camera to snap some pictures of the momentous occasion.

As strains of "You'll Never Walk Alone" played over the sound system, I swallowed the lump in my throat and began to walk down the bleachers to get a closer shot. I thought of all the storms my daughter and I had braved together over the years. As I stepped down, closer and closer to Rachel, I heard, "... And don't be afraid of the dark. At the end of the storm is a golden sky ..."

Thump, thump, thump, thump, thump. CLUNK.

"OUCH!"

I had tripped and fallen down about five bleacher steps, reaching the bottom in a final and most undignified thud. My ankle was bleeding, my camera was lying on the ground, and every eye was turned in my direction. I gave a brave little wave to assure everyone I was fine; then I reached for my camera and snapped a picture of my daughter who was staring into the lens like a deer caught in the headlights.

~

Rachel and I are still opposites — she's neat and aware; I'm messy and forgetful. She has become a vegan; I love butter and bacon. She grasps technology immediately and knows the purpose of every button on her smart phone, while I still answer my smart phone upside down half the time. (Many of our phone conversations start with my saying, "I can't hear you very well!" Rachel patiently answers in what sounds like a tiny, far away voice, "Mom, turn your phone around!")

We are totally simpatico on at least two fronts, however. First, we love stories that make us laugh, and second, we love good home cooking.

On a recent visit, within minutes after our hugs and greetings, Rachel and I pounced on our favorite topic: "What'll we cook and eat?" I had recently perfected my own Italian Puttanesca Sauce with a kick of Texas heat. I suggested I whip up a batch to serve over whole-grain angel-hair pasta. "Perfect," Rach said, combing through my pantry to check out the rations.

"Aha!" she said. "Garbanzo beans! Can I roast them to put in the sauce?"

A vegan for a year and a half at that point, Rachel had turned into a great cook. She really knew her way around legumes and fresh produce.

"Go for it," I said. "I need some new recipes to get more veggies into our diet."

I watched with mama pride as she deftly rinsed the beans and patted them dry, tossed them with olive oil, salt, pepper, garlic, smoked paprika, and poured them onto a cookie sheet. Then she popped them in the oven like a confident younger, prettier, way-more-petite Julia Child.

This cooperative lunch soon had us rolling our eyes toward heaven and high-fiving each other across the table.

"Oh, ymmmmm ...," she said.

"Uh hummm ...," I agreed.

The garbanzos were delightfully toasty with a crunchy, smoky crust that was perfectly paired with the thick, tangy Italian sauce.

"Cha-ching, Rachey." I smiled in approval, savoring another bite.

And at that moment it was as if I could hear the encouraging cheers of all the great women from all the family kitchens I've known all my life.

~

My grandmother Nonny resembled the kindest version of Mrs. Santa Claus you've ever seen in any children's book: silver hair piled up in a French twist, blue eyes twinkling, ever aproned and stirring at something fragrant on her old 1940s gas stove. Usually it was a pot of black-eyed peas or red beans seasoned with a salty ham hock, but sometimes (glory!) it was the vanilla custard for my favorite childhood dessert: banana pudding.

My mother often reminded me of Lucille Ball. She kept her red hair (from a bottle, like Lucy's) swept up in a French twist, and she wore pretty dresses with cinched waists. She was funny and loved to laugh, providing both entertainment and an appreciative audience for us kids. She has always been beautiful and kept an eye on her girlish figure by eating regular servings of the ever-popular "diet plate" of the '70s: a lean hamburger patty, cottage cheese, and a slice of canned pineapple, usually with a side of Tab or Fresca. But every Saturday she would bake a decadent cake that we'd drool over and snack on all weekend long.

There was a four-layer Fresh Coconut Cake that had to sit for four agonizingly tempting days in the fridge so the fresh-grated-coconut-sour-cream-and-sugar frosting could sweeten and thicken into the ambrosia of angels. Sometimes she'd make a classic Italian Cream Cake, rich with toasted pecans, coconut, and cream cheese. There was a moist chocolate cake frosted with a boiled icing that tasted like homemade fudge, and a doctored-from-a mix cake made with cinnamon and sour cream and baked in a Bundt pan, called Sock-It-to-Me Cake. The Saturday cakes ceased to exist sometime in the 1980s when mom discovered that sugar was doing evil things to her body. Still, she baked deliciously, just more healthily. Though it's not coconut or chocolate cake, I love her recipe for moist and healthy Oat and Fruit Gem Muffins made with oats, dried fruit, nuts, and bananas. They allow me to indulge in sweets and feel smug about it at the same time.

If my mother was Queen of Cakes, her big sister, my Aunt Etta, was Empress of Pies. From the edges of my memory, I can see my Aunt Etta, a statuesque beauty in her fitted dress and heels, standing next to Nonny, putting the final swirls of whipped cream on her famous chocolate pie. (Her filling was smooth as silk milk chocolate, with a generous pour of fragrant vanilla.)

In addition to baking the best pies I've ever tasted, Aunt Etta was the first writer in the family. I'll never forget the pride I felt as a thirteen-year-old, watching her sign copies of her book, *Help Is Only a Prayer Away*, at a book party at the Sweetwater, Texas, library. Aunt Etta noted my mother's talent for writing and encouraged her efforts as well. Before long, my mom was pounding away at the typewriter, publishing articles and collaborating on books.

Over the years, my mother passed the humor-cooking-writing torch on to me and my younger sister. Cooking and serving alongside Mother gave me the skills needed to start a part-time catering business that helped pay the bills in lean times. The writing lessons and appreciation for humor she gave me would launch what would be a full decade of speaking, entertaining, and writing. My sister too, for whom my daughter is named, has written and published three books of humor and inspiration.

It is interesting to me how many of my writing friends, and great writers, also love to cook and have an appreciation for fine food. Anne Morrow Lindbergh once wrote, "When I cannot write a poem, I bake biscuits and feel just as pleased." Perhaps there's some mysterious link between the writing and cooking gene.

Now I am warmed to see my daughter pick up the legacy of laughter, love of cooking, and the ability to tell and write a good story with the best of the women in our family tree. In truth, I have known that Rachel had The Gift since she was a teenager. I just didn't know when she would be ready to see it, embrace it, and share it.

The apostle Paul told his apprentice Timothy about the importance of "fanning into flame" the gift of God within him, emphasizing that this gift was passed down from his grandmother and his mother. The word picture that leaps to my mind when I read these words is my Nonny putting her arm around my Aunt Etta and my mother, my mother putting her arms around me and my sister, and now me putting my arm around my own daughter to pass along whatever we have to give one another so that each woman may use these gifts, in her own unique way, to better enjoy and bless the world.

~

My cell phone rang breaking my reverie. It was Rachel.

"Mom, how did you know? I didn't even know! I just took a pregnancy test. I'm going to have a baby!"

FAVORITE FAMILY RECIPES
Becky and Rachel's Spicy Puttanesca Sauce

After making this dish together, we thought, "Wouldn't it be great if we could share a kitchen more often, despite one of us living in Texas and the other in Colorado?" Thus the idea for our virtual kitchen at www.welaughwecrywecook.com was born and eventually led to this book, another extension of our kitchens to yours.

Serves 4.

½ cup chopped onion

2 cloves minced garlic

2 tablespoons olive oil

1 cup chopped vegetables (broccoli, zucchini, squash, eggplant, carrots, whatever you've got on hand)

½ cup marinated artichoke hearts, quartered

1 tablespoon capers or 2 tablespoon olives (any variety), pitted and chopped

2 tablespoons pesto sauce (optional, but toss it in if you have it on hand)

2 tablespoons pepperoncini peppers, diced

2 tablespoons sun-dried tomatoes, diced

1–2 tablespoons brown sugar

1 28-ounce can crushed tomatoes with basil and garlic

1 teaspoon Italian seasoning or oregano

⅛ teaspoon salt and pepper (or to taste)

16 ounces dry pasta, cooked per package instructions

Optional: ½ pound of cooked ground beef and ½ pound cooked Italian sausage, or 1 can garbanzo beans, roasted (see instructions)

In a medium-hot skillet, sauté onion and garlic in olive oil for 2 minutes. Add other vegetables; cook about 5 more minutes. Add remaining ingredients except spices and pasta. Turn heat to medium high. Stir and simmer until sauce is thick and chunky. Stir in optional meat or garbanzo beans. Season with salt, pepper, and Italian spices to taste. Add more brown sugar if more sweetness is desired. Simmer 5 more minutes. Serve atop pasta.

To Roast Garbanzo Beans: Heat oven to 400°. Rinse garbanzos (also called chickpeas) and pat dry. On baking pan, mix garbanzos with 1 tablespoon olive oil, 1 teaspoon balsamic vinegar, 1 teaspoon Italian seasonings (we love McCormick's Italian Herb Seasoning Grinder), and ¼ teaspoon sea salt. Roast for 10 minutes, shaking the pan a couple of times during the cooking. (You can also do this on the stove top over medium heat for 5–7 minutes, shaking every minute.) Check for seasoning; sprinkle with more salt or balsamic if desired.

- *Vegetarian (leave out meat))*
- *Vegan friendly (leave out meat; use dairy-free pesto or just omit it)*
- *Gluten free (substitute pasta with spaghetti squash or gluten-free pasta, like the ones made of quinoa, corn, or rice)*

Aunt Etta's Chocolate Pie

This pie is more milk chocolate than dark chocolate. You may have never tasted a pie quite like this, but once you do, you'll never forget it. This family treasure is written exactly as my Aunt Etta gave it to me, back when phones had "hooks." —*Becky*

Makes filling for two 9-inch cream pies.

4 cups whole milk, heated until hot but not boiling (you can do this in the microwave to speed things up if you like)

1¾ cups sugar

3 tablespoons cocoa

½ cup plus 1 tablespoon and 1 teaspoon more of flour

3 egg yolks

1 teaspoon vanilla

2 baked and cooled 9-inch pie shells (I like mine a little on the brown and crispy side, as they are less inclined to get soggy.)

In a saucepan, combine hot milk with sugar, cocoa, and flour. Cook for 10 minutes, stirring constantly as it thickens. (*Becky's note:* I use a heat-proof spatula for stirring.)

Beat egg yolks until foamy in a small bowl. Add 2 to 3 tablespoons of hot mixture from saucepan to yolks to temper them; then add this back to the pan. Cook again until very thick, at least 5 minutes, stirring occasionally. (I take my phone off the hook.) This is your most important step. The mixture will seem thick enough after one minute, but if the yolks are not cooked thoroughly, after the custard is cold it breaks down and runs.

Take off heat and add 1 teaspoon vanilla. Never put a lid on the mixture while it is cooling. The "sweat" that accumulates on lid will be absorbed back into the custard and cause it to break down and become runny. Just stir the mixture occasionally to keep it from running or pour it directly into the pie crusts and allow it to cool there, and don't worry about a film over the top. That tastes good too.

Top with whatever you prefer: meringue, Cool Whip, or real whipped cream.

· *Vegetarian*

Granny's Oat and Fruit Gems

These make healthy snacks and great grab-'n'-go breakfasts.

Serves 18.

  2 bananas, mashed

  2 peeled apples, grated

  3 cups old fashioned oats

  ½ teaspoon sea salt

  ½ cup raw organic sugar

  ½ cup dried chopped fruit (dates, dried cranberries, coconut, raisins, apricots all work well)

  1 cup nuts and/or seeds, chopped (walnuts, pecans, almonds, sunflower seeds all work well)

  ½ teaspoon almond extract (or 1 teaspoon vanilla)

  grated zest of one orange

Preheat oven to 350°. Mix all of the above together in a large mixing bowl. Spray or oil muffin pans. Fill them about ⅔ full and gently press down with back of spoon. Bake for 20 to 30 minutes or until just golden brown around edges and top. When cool to touch, gently remove from pan.

  · *Vegan/vegetarian*
  · *Gluten-free friendly (use gluten-free oats)*

Four-Day Coconut Cake

This cake is so simple to make, just hard to wait to eat! It is perfect, however, for holidays because you can make it ahead of time and forget about it until it is time to serve. It's so pretty at Christmas and Easter, especially. It gets very moist as the cake soaks up some of the yummy frosting. Slices and serves "like a dream," my mother Ruthie says. —Becky

Serves 16 slices.

Day 1

  2 cups sour cream

  1 cup sugar

  2 12-ounce packages frozen coconut (This can be tough to find but is usually near the frozen fruit in small flat packages. It is easiest to find in Southern states or Asian markets. If you find it, it makes a remarkably fresh-tasting cake. If you can't find the frozen coconut, use 4 lightly packed cups of a moist packaged pre-sweetened coconut instead, and cut sugar back to ½ cup.)

Day 2

  1 package yellow cake mix, baked according to directions in two greased and floured 9-inch round cake pans

Combine sour cream, sugar, and frozen coconut in a large bowl and let sit overnight. The next day bake the yellow cakes and cool. Carefully flip the cakes out of the pans and cut each round into two layers, leaving four layers total. You can use a thread, tied around the cake evenly, then pull both ends and it "cuts" the cake for you! Ice the cake using all the coconut mixture between layers on top and all around. Wrap cake with plastic wrap and leave in fridge for at least 3 days; 4 is even better.

  • Vegetarian

Chapter 2

I Say "Tomato"; She Says, "Did I Burn It?"

A messy kitchen is a happy kitchen
and this kitchen is delirious.
unattributed

RACHEL

People sometimes ask me how I got my skill for organizing things. I tell them the truth, "Organization was my form of teenage rebellion."

Though we've all heard exasperated moms tell stories of their messy kids who misplace library books and lose their homework, I grew up with a mother who was as forgetful as Dory from *Finding Nemo* and as messy as Cookie Monster. Thankfully, like Dory and Cookie Monster, she was also usually pretty funny and cute and loving, which helped calm the aggravation factor somewhat. So instead of her asking me if I remembered my lunch or backpack on the way to school, I would be the one asking her if she remembered her purse and keys. She was forever putting her lipstick on without a mirror, and I was forever wiping away the clown-smile edges that overlapped her actual lips, and I would rub in the two dots of lipstick she dapped on her cheeks for a quick rosy hue but had forgotten to blend in.

The upshot of being raised by an ADD mother was that I learned a lot about self-sufficiency at a young age. I grew up in the country with three brothers whose clothes seemed always covered in dirt from fishing or hunting or working, so the laundry room was a perpetual challenge for Mom. There were always baskets full of miscellaneous clothes, and once a family of hissing possums moved in to claim the laundry room as their new home. By the time I was in fourth grade—I took control: I washed my own clothes (whites, darks, and lights separately), and had a system in place so that I would never wear the same outfit in any three-week stretch. By ninth grade, I shopped for and made my own healthy lunch and breakfast every day: a peanut-butter sandwich before cross-country practice; a banana-and-chocolate SlimFast for my "locker room" breakfast; a package of light tuna salad with five crackers (no more, no less), and an apple for lunch. No wonder I was so thin back then. On top of running five miles every morning and having a fifteen-year-old's metabolism, I ate like a bird. I did, however, eat plenty of sixteen-layer lasagna, creamy gorgonzola pasta, and Italian bread dipped in olive oil and toasted garlic after my shifts as a hostess at an Italian restaurant.

My idea of a balanced diet has definitely evolved over the years.

All this to say that my proclivity to cleanliness and organization, and Mom's to walk through the world in a ditzy fog, leaving a trail of cookie crumbs behind her, sometimes led to a bit of role reversal.

In a childhood version of "the grass is always greener on the other side," I envied my friend Cricket Cowley, who, despite having been nicknamed after an insect, had a normal mother, whom I called Miss Janice. We often spent the night at each other's houses, and on school mornings, Miss Janice would tiptoe into Cricket's pale-pink room with pretty porcelain dolls lined up on white shelves. She'd gently pat Cricket's back. "Breakfast is ready, girls," she'd say in her sweet, small voice. "Come on, Crickie, time to wake up." Cricket would pull the soft floral quilt over her head and bury her face into her feather pillow. "I'm noooot hungry," she would moan.

I, on the other hand, would eagerly toss off the freshly washed sheets and hop out of her antique frame bed, pulling my hair back in a quick ponytail. "Cricket, how can you sleep through the smell of homemade sausage gravy?"

Eventually, after a couple more lilting wake-up calls from Miss Janice, Cricket would crawl out of bed, and we would climb onto the cushy stools at the breakfast bar. Waiting for us were two small glasses with orange slices painted on them, filled with juice. Miss Janice would put a plate full of fluffy biscuits in front of each of us and then ladle on the sausage gravy. As we ate, she read a short *Daily Bread* devotion and prayed for our day.

Mom has never been a morning person, and my dad usually left early for work, so at our house we were mostly on our own in the mornings. A peaceful morning meant no one shouted above 120 decibels. My older brother, Zeke, sometimes made pancakes for breakfast, but since he loved to experiment, he never made anything "plain" and never cooked without using every pan and utensil in the kitchen (a trait he inherited from our mother). Then as soon as he served us, he'd declare, "I cooked. Y'all clean."

He was determined that we all taste his "breakfast creations." He once chased me around with something vile on the end of a fork, a piece of pancake that smelled of peanut butter and fish. With Sam-I-Am persistence he begged me to take, "Just one bite, Rach. Try it!" I need to pause here to explain how hard it is to say no to Zeke when he's pumped up about an idea. Using the tactics of a hard-pitch time-share salesman, Zeke would convince me that his latest culinary creation was "a delicacy in many countries," or some such thing, and I'd reluctantly take a bite to get him off my back. "It's good, right?" he'd say eagerly even as I was spitting it out in the sink. His creativity and persistence eventually paid off. He is now an architect in Denver, building his dream home in the mountains with his dream girl and their two wildly creative and persistent boys.

At 7:30 a.m., I'd start rounding up my brothers. "Come on, I cannot be late again!" From her bedroom Mom would mumble something resembling, "Bye. Love you. Have a good day!" We'd head out the door, Gabe and I piling into Zeke's old stick-shift Chevy Blazer. (Zach, my oldest brother, was grown and out of the house at this point.) Looking back, some of my fondest memories of my brothers are of those hectic, hurried mornings, driving to school with the windows down, all three of us belting out songs to Rusted Root from Zeke's indie music collection. "Send me on my way; send me on my-y-y-y way!" With Mom out of commission before 8:00 a.m., we really learned to take care of each other.

After school, I often rode the bus home with Cricket to her house. She had a daily chore to complete before Miss Janice got home from her job as a school nurse. I would help with her chores so we could go play or watch TV sooner. One time, Cricket was mopping the floors quickly and hastily when Miss Janice walked in and admonished, "Remember to mop in sections, Cricket, going one direction and then over again in the opposite direction."

"Like this?" Cricket asked, pushing her mop in random circles and winking at me.

"No, no, no, I'll show you again." Miss Janice grabbed the mop and proceeded to "demonstrate how it is done" on the rest of the kitchen while Cricket hid her grin and pretended to take notes.

On the other hand, our house was like a perpetual Spring Break vacation for Cricket. An incredibly imaginative tomboy, her creative heart longed for a haven free of chore charts and the color pink. When we'd arrive at my house after school, we'd toss our backpacks full of homework on the floor and scrounge the fridge for whatever we could find: cooked frozen pizzas dipped in Ranch dressing, boxed mac and cheese, ramen noodles, or our favorite (and only) "recipe," scrambled egg and mayonnaise sandwiches.

Cricket loved doing impersonations, and my mom thought they were hilarious, which, of course, pleased Cricket no end. After a quick snack and a chat with Mom at the kitchen counter,

Cricket's big imagination would have us jumping from beam to beam on one of my dad's unfinished construction projects around the house, pretending we were homeless kids running from cops in a warehouse or members of a grunge band shooting a music video. To a right-brained creative type, our home must have seemed like a dream come true. As one of my brother's friends wrote in a note to my mom, "I love coming to y'all's house ... because there's nothing we can do to mess it up."

Cricket and I often joked that we were switched at birth, but truthfully, neither of us would trade our moms or our childhoods for anything. What a boring life I would have led without my Dora and Cookie Monster. And Cricket and my mom may have never made it anywhere on time without Miss Janice and me watching the clock and nudging them out the door. I guess God knows ADDs and OCDs need each other, which is why they so often end up in the same family ... or marriage.

Now that I had a baby of my own on the way, I couldn't help but wonder if my child would grow up to be an organized person like me, loading the dishwasher with the precision of a lab scientist; or would my darling child be a Messy, like my mom, loading the dishwasher with all the finesse of a drunk monkey?

I'm guessing from the law of averages, that I'll likely produce scatterbrained, messy offspring, at some point. This worries me some. And yet, I look back on Mom's life and realize that because of her sense of humor, no mess, mishap, or forgetful episode went to waste. Somehow it all got turned into a batter of material and came out of the "creative oven" in book or kitchen table story form, making us laugh.

Eventually.

To be clear, my mother knew how to cook (thanks to the good home cooks she grew up with). When she put her mind to it and focused on the task at hand, she was often a *great* cook. (Though her standards of kitchen cleanliness have never been pristine, and she'll use the juice from a lime that looks like a kiwi without giving it a second thought, something I would never do. Still, to her credit, or divine protection, she never gave us food poisoning.) Mom's culinary challenges mostly occurred when her brain was occupied with chasing us four kids, her return to college in her mid-thirties, then a stint at teaching first grade, followed by a writing and speaking career. At some point while Mom was preparing a meal, with all this activity going on, her forgetfulness would inevitably kick in, and as a result, Mom's kitchen disasters alone could fill a book. (And indeed, this book is padded with several of them.)

We were talking and laughing about some of her earlier cooking "challenges" recently on the phone, and I urged her to write them down as a way to encourage women to understand that being a good and gracious cook and hostess does not happen overnight. And that, in fact, if she could pull it off, just about anybody could. She's now known in her Denver circles as the local "Paula Deen," often throwing together impromptu meals for two or twenty with Southern grace. Her cooking skills took a serious leap forward after she married Greg, who has a real appreciation for regular home-cooked meals. Without children under foot, she had more time to practice and perfect recipes, and a little more brain space to focus. These days my adult siblings and I love "going home to Mama's" for a home-cooked meal and always feel pampered, loved, and well-fed around her kitchen table. But trust me, this was not always the case. My mother is living testimony to this truth: As long as you keep a sense of humor and a fire extinguisher handy, you really don't need to worry about perfection in the kitchen. And that no matter how young or old you are, there is always hope for improvement.

Little did I know how much I'd need to remember that motherhood—with all the distractions, exhaustion, and forgetfulness that comes with the title—can really put a dent in high standards of homemaking.

BECKY

First, perhaps a word of explanation about my Messy Brain Condition is in order (for those of you who are either a Messy or struggling to live with one). A few years ago, as research for a collaborative book about the brain, I had a brain scan done at the Amen Clinic. The good news is, contrary to urban myth, I do indeed have a brain! In fact, according to Dr. Daniel Amen, world renowned brain expert: I have a "beautiful brain." No dementia or shrinkage of vital thinking tissues. On my brain scan, however, there is what appears to be a dent right in front of my forehead. This is not an actual hole in my head, but an indication that blood flow is in no hurry to infuse my Prefrontal Cortex with thinking fluid. The result is that I've gone through my entire life with something called Inattentive ADD. It basically means that though I am a bright and creative thinker, I am simultaneously ditzy and absentminded, at least when it comes to remembering things like time and appointments and where I put my glasses or getting jokes, which mostly fly over my head at the speed of light.

Through the years, I've amassed a wide variety of experiences resulting in the following tips that I thought might come in handy for focus-challenged cooks like me.

Tips for My Fellow Absentminded Gourmets

1. Lids Matter

Who knew it? Though they are next to impossible to keep up with, lids are actually essential kitchen items. I discovered this in a variety of interesting ways.

There was the time I enthusiastically wound up my Cuisinart salad spinner, a gift from my efficient salad-loving daughter. What I did not do was read the instructions, which I'm now guessing said something like, "Wait until the inner whirling colander comes to a complete halt before removing the lid." If you remove the lid early in the spinning process, I can testify that you will immediately give your entire kitchen, including ceiling and floor, a certain lettuce-based Rain Forest look. (A side note: if you ever happen to walk away from a whirling mixer full of mashed potatoes to answer the phone in the other room, upon your return it will look as if your kitchen has just been freshly decorated by Dr. Seuss, with whimsical blobs of mashed potato "snow" adorning everything in sight.)

I also have the strange habit of, apparently, throwing lids away without realizing it. I don't remember doing it, and I don't mean to do it. But there must be an Inner Lid Tosser in my complex psyche that opens up jars and bottles, then immediately walks sleep-walker-like to the trash can and tosses the lids away.

When I married Greg nine years ago, he was perplexed by this little quirk of mine. He asked me nicely to try to remember to put the lid back on the milk carton, because he really preferred that our dairy products not taste and smell like yesterday's tuna casserole. Eventually I assumed that my memory must have taken the hint because lids started regularly appearing on the cartons and bottles and jars in the fridge. One day, however, I opened a drawer to find it filled with lids, lids, lids, and more lids. Lids of every conceivable shape and size. I looked at Greg, and he simply smiled and said, "At one point I realized that you were incapable of *not* throwing lids away, so rather than continue to lecture and make you feel bad, or put up with a lidless life, I adjusted. I just began saving lids. And when you throw one away, I put one from the 'lid drawer' back on. Simple solution."

In a story to be filed under, "Help! I'm turning into my mother!" Rachel called the other day and said, "Mom, I just found out that Jared and Greg have yet one more thing in common."

"What's that?" I asked.

"Yesterday, Jared asked me why I always tie a knot in the bread bag, why I don't use the little twist ties that come with it. I had to tell him the truth: I had no idea. I just know that, growing up, I don't ever remember seeing a twist tie on a loaf of bread unless it was brand new. Now, I'm guessing you threw them away without thinking, and so, all these years, I've been doing the same thing because it never occurred to me that twist ties are there to be reused."

"That's so funny," I said, glancing over at our own knotted bag of bread by the toaster.

"And that's not all. Next, Jared opened a drawer, showing me his 'stash' of twist ties that he'd been patiently putting on the bread bags all these years, just quietly hoping I'd get the hint and change my knotting habit."

God bless our patient, adaptable men.

Last night I was making sliced, round oven fries when two lidless items (even Greg can't keep up with *all* the lids I lose) fell out of the cabinet and onto the pan: some Cajun Spice (it worked) and a small bottle of blue food coloring. Going with Julia Child's admonition to, "Never apologize, never explain," I went ahead and served the blue-hued chips for dinner, calling them the Blue Plate Special.

Postscript: As I was in the process of editing this chapter, the most unusual thing happened. After taking a bath, I went to the kitchen for a cup of water, as is my nightly habit, then to the bedroom where I rubbed lotion on my feet before tucking them under the covers and going to bed. Suddenly, my feet were on *fire*. I could not imagine the problem, but I went to the bathroom to get a washcloth, wiped the lotion off (which seemed to cool them immediately) then padded back through the kitchen, reapplied lotion, and got into bed. Within seconds, my feet were ablaze again. I went to the kitchen, switched on a light and saw the culprit. Same can of Cajun Spice from the above story, with same missing lid, was again lying at an angle in an open cabinet, spilling its contents over the floor, which I had then walked on. So

basically, I'd been rubbing cayenne pepper into my feet throughout the mysterious evening. Don't you hate it when that happens
to you?

2. On Burnt Offerings

I hate to admit it, but it's true. For many years the smoke alarm
was basically my kids' dinner bell.

As Rachel pointed out, though I'm a truly good cook, I'm still
not always an alert cook, which means that I tend to burn food. A
lot. Once, my then-teenage son Zach walked through the kitchen
where I'd just overcooked something in the oven. Through the
billowing smoke he nonchalantly commented, "Mmmm, smells
like mom's home cooking!"

When Zeke was about five years old, I handed him a perfectly golden piece of toast. He took the toast and a dinner knife
and walked over to the trash can and started scraping it. "Zeke,
honey," I said, "you don't have to scrape your toast today. Mommy
didn't burn it!" To which he looked at me, eyes wide, and said,
"Oh, I thought we always had to whittle our toast." Bless his heart,
he just thought this was standard toast-eating procedure.

Rachel and I were recently browsing the food memoir section
at Barnes & Noble, doing a little research for this book. I opened
to page one of a memoir called *Toast: The Story of a Boy's Hunger* by
English food writer Nigel Slater and laughed. I called Rachel over
and had her read it, as well. (Good snippets in books are like tasty
bites of food. I want to share them impulsively and immediately
with someone I love.) Slater wrote:

> My mother burns the toast as surely as the sun rises each
> morning. In fact, I doubt that she's ever made a round of toast
> in her life that failed to fill the kitchen with plumes of throat-
> catching smoke. I am nine now, and have never seen butter
> without black bits in it.
>
> It is impossible not to love someone who makes toast for
> you.[2]

"Yes," my adult daughter agreed, looking up from the page and smiling at me. "That is true. It is impossible not to love you." Then she added, "Plus, I know how to disable a shrieking smoke alarm in record time."

To absentminded mothers everywhere, let this be an encouragement to you.

3. Remember: Garnish Food; Accessorize People

I throw this short tidbit in here just in case any of you are apt to toss your jewelry, cell phones, or hair clips into any old bowl lying around your kitchen. I once delivered a nice salad to a neighbor friend who was recovering from an illness. Melissa called, laughing. "Becky, I just tossed the salad and to my surprise, a pair of loop earrings emerged along with the tomatoes and cucumbers." Let this be a lesson to you: check your bowls for rogue jewelry before filling them with food and sharing with friends. (Three days after writing this memory, I presented a tray of cookies to some of Greg's coworkers. One of them, looking both confused and amused, grabbed a cookie that had one of my stray earrings attached to it. I'd been looking everywhere for it.)

4. When Food Goes Missing

This is a common problem with forgetful cooks. You have a bowl of apples, perhaps, right there in front of you, ready to be peeled. But the next thing you know, you turn your back for a moment or get a little caught up in a story on TV, then you look back on the counter and the apples are simply ... gone. I have learned from years of experience that these mysterious food items are most likely to show up in one of the following places: the oven, the dishwasher, or the pantry. It never hurts to check the washing machine. Or your purse.

The biggest food item that I ever misplaced was an industrial-size plastic pan of raw marinating pork chops. The kids were young, our budget small, so I'd taken a job as a part-time food caterer. The lakeside clubhouse where I worked was just a block from our home, so in many ways it was a great gig. I was always going in a dozen directions, however, and my poor memory would take quite a hit. One night I prepared a dinner for about twenty people. But about two hours before serving time, after checking all the usual suspicious places, the pork chops seemed to have mysteriously evaporated. I finally convinced myself that I probably just dreamed them up, that they may have never actually existed.

Using a backup plan (absentminded cooks—especially if you are a caterer—must *always* have a backup plan), I quickly seared a couple of huge beef tenderloins instead. While the tenderloins were finishing up in the oven, one of the guests popped her head into the kitchen saying, "Becky, we were all admiring your ... uh, interesting centerpiece in front of the fireplace." I followed her to the gathering room of the clubhouse, and there on the coffee table, surrounded by flowers and candles, backlit by the glow of the hearth, was the enormous plastic gray pan, filled with twenty raw pork chops floating in brown marinade. Thankfully, this group of twenty knew me well and spent the rest of the evening chuckling about the incident.

Rose Dodson was my personal assistant for several years when my writing and speaking career was at full throttle. She looked like her name, a golden haired beauty who seemed to appear from another place and time. But Rose was no delicate flower in the brain compartment. She is and was as sharp as Sherlock. My parents once stopped by my home to join us for lunch, and we'd just spent a good twenty minutes searching the house for a missing loaf of bread I'd just purchased, with the plan to make sandwiches. Rose walked into the kitchen, and my parents asked, "Rose, if you were Becky, where would you have placed a loaf of bread?" Without hesitation, Rose walked to the microwave, opened it, and handed them a loaf of Wonder. To this day they speak of Rose with something akin to pure awe, as they should.

~

I wish I could say that all those crazy, absentminded adventures are a part of my history, but ADD is a gift that keeps on giving. (How will my children ever know if I've got age-related memory loss or am just being myself? I have no clue. I could slip into senility and it would go completely undetected for years.) I drove through a Taco Bell this morning, famished after a workout (which may be why I'm not losing weight at warp speed). I placed my order, but the voice on the intercom sounded confused. So I repeated it, carefully: "A taco and a small Coke, please." Still she sounded flummoxed, and that's when I looked at the menu sign and realized I was at a Starbucks drive-through. I shared this on Facebook and received the most wonderful comments, like "Did you change your order to a Taco Frappucino?" and "You crack me up." But the best was from a friend who is struggling to beat perfectionism; she said, "Oh, Becky, you make my life worth living."

It has long been my motto that if you cannot get your act together (and I've given it a good fifty-year try), then the least you can do is try to make your act entertaining. Sometimes our unique gift to the world is to help other people feel better about themselves simply because we exist, continually scraping off the burnt edges of life and serving it up with sides of apologies, love, and laughter.

~

An aside to moms of all ages: Even Iron Chefs have bad days in the kitchen. And being a mom is a little like being an Iron Chef—with a million things to do in a ridiculously short amount of time —only you have to do it without a full night's sleep or hired help.

There are no perfect cooks and no perfect mothers. You will try. You will try so very hard. Still you will fail and fall and sometimes flail. You will feel guilty about all this. When I read about

Rachel's younger self longing for order and neatness, for a mother who valued routines and was fully awake and aware in the morning, I ache with the yearning to go back in time and do it all better. If only I cooked beautiful breakfasts and kept a better house, I think, perhaps my children would never have suffered, never have any of their own personality quirks, never made their own share of mistakes. If I had been more perfect, perhaps they would also be perfect and have only perfect things happen to them.

But let me share something my mother, Ruthie, shared with me. Perhaps it will comfort you as it has comforted me through the years. "No matter how well you do your job as a parent, even if you should do it almost perfectly, you'll still raise little human beings with selfish streaks, temper tantrums, and the remarkable ability to lie to you with the face of an angel. And even if you could be a perfect parent, your child will still have to grow up in an imperfect world and live through their own share of disappointments and heartaches. Ultimately, you need God's grace and they'll need God's grace, and that's just the way it is."

So try not to sweat your imperfections. We are just fallible human beings doing our best to raise other fallible human beings. Do your best with the big stuff, and trust that loads of love and laughter and grace will cover the rest.

On your deathbed your adult kids won't remember how you loaded the dishwasher (okay, maybe mine will as it is a memorable sort of thing); they'll remember that you thought they were remarkable, lovable, and capable — a blessing to you and others. If you do your job as well as you can, you will arrive at old age knowing you and your children both had your share of flaws and mistakes, but you'll focus on what matters most — how, over the scraping sound of burnt toast being whittled, you loved each other to the moon and back.

FOOLPROOF RECIPES
FOR THE DISTRACTED HOME COOK
Caramelized Toast

"Salted caramel" is all the rage, and this quick 'n' easy toast, with its combination of melted butter and brown sugar, creates a wonderful sweet-salty-caramelly tasting treat. A nice alternative to cinnamon toast on a chilly morning or for an after-school snack. — *Becky*

1 Serving.

> 1 slice bread, any kind you like
>
> 1–2 teaspoons salted butter
>
> 1 tablespoon brown sugar (may use less for smaller pieces of bread)

Spread a slice of bread generously with butter. Sprinkle with brown sugar, all the way to the edges.

Broil about 4 inches from heat until brown sugar has melted and starts to bubble. Remove; let cool a bit. Cut into triangles (I use kitchen shears) and serve.

- Vegetarian
- Vegan (substitute vegan margarine such as Earth Balance)
- Gluten free (use gluten-free bread)

Sweet and Spicy Oven "Blackened" Tilapia

Imagine my delight when "blackened food" became popular among food lovers. Of course, "blackening" doesn't really mean "burnt"; it comes from the heating of spices onto a piece of meat until a flavorful crust is formed. This sweet–smoky, spicy blackened tilapia is not only full of flavor, but it cooks in no time at all. I make it at least once a month. Rachel loves making a vegan version, using Earth Balance instead of butter and tofu slices instead of fish. — Becky

Serves 2.

> 2 tablespoons olive oil
>
> 2 tablespoons butter
>
> 4 medium to large tilapia fillets
>
> 2 tablespoons smoked paprika
>
> 2 tablespoons cumin
>
> 3 tablespoons brown sugar
>
> salt and pepper
>
> 1 lemon, cut in half

Pre-heat oven to 350°. Put oil and butter in rectangle pan (large enough to hold tilapia without overlapping) and put in oven until butter has melted. Tilt pan until it is evenly coated. In small bowl, mix paprika, cumin, and brown sugar. Lightly salt and pepper both sides of 4 fillets. Lay tilapia fillets side by side in the buttery pan. Turn over so both sides are coated with oil/butter. Generously sprinkle tops of tilapia with the brown sugar-spice mix (using all of it), patting it in gently. Squeeze one half lemon over all. Put in oven for 15 minutes or until fish flakes easily. Then turn oven to broil and, watching carefully, broil the tops of the fish until the spice mixture starts to caramelize. Remove and serve with the remaining lemon half; cut in pretty slices as garnish.

- *Vegetarian (sub a block of tofu gently pressed to remove excess water and sliced into four "fillets")*
- *Vegan (sub vegan margarine such as Earth Balance)*
- *Gluten free*

Tomato Basil Stackers

*This is one of my favorite summer snacks when basil is growing
like a weed and tomatoes are vibrant red, sweet, and juicy. During
that short season, I've been known to eat it every day for weeks. The
combination of avocado, garlic, and basil is like an Italian flavor
explosion in your mouth. Also, the presentation is lovely and cheery
and simply makes me happy. It would be perfect for a summer brunch
or done in smaller open-faced stacks as an Italian dinner appetizer, a
vertical tomato bruschetta of sorts. —Rachel*

Serves 1.

1 whole-grain English muffin, split in half (I especially like
    the Ezekiel 4:9 brand)

1 garlic clove, minced

1 tablespoon olive oil

3 slices of vine-ripened tomato

6 fresh basil leaves, gently torn

½ avocado, pitted and sliced

salt

fresh cracked pepper

drizzle of high-quality olive oil

Turn your oven on low broil. In a small bowl, mix olive oil with
minced garlic. Spread garlic and oil on the inner side of the English
muffin slices. Place directly on the top rack of your oven and
broil until it's light brown and crispy (about 1 minute). Slightly
smash the avocado onto the toasted English muffin halves. Then
on one of the halves, layer two basil leaves and a tomato slice
three times, sprinkling with salt, fresh cracked pepper, and a small
drizzle of high-quality olive oil after each tomato slice. Top with
the other half of the English muffin.

· Vegan/vegetarian
· Gluten free (use gluten-free bread)

Warm Stuffed Dates

With just two ingredients, dates and almonds, and done in under two minutes, this is almost not a recipe, but they are so delightful I had to share them. When warmed, the inside of the dates get soft and gooey, like rich caramel. Wrapped around crunchy almonds, they make a healthy two-bite dessert, an energizing anytime snack, or an elegant party appetizer guests go nuts over. —Rachel

Serves 1

> 1 Medjool date
>
> 2–3 roasted almonds (I love the oil roasted, unsalted ones, if you can find them)

Turn oven to broil. Cut a slit down the side of the date and pop the pit out. Generously stuff dates with 2 to 3 almonds and reseal the slit (dates are sticky, so it just sticks back together). Broil for 1 minute; flip them and broil for 30–60 more seconds. Let cool slightly before serving. (Easily distracted cooks prone to burning things under the broiler can cook these at 350° for 5–10 minutes if preferred.)

- Vegan/vegetarian
- Gluten free

Chapter 3

Diet for a Small Palate

Cooking is like love.
It should be entered into with abandon
or not at all.
Harriet Van Horne

BECKY

I love variety in my life when it comes to food. The more exotic, the better. The more spice, the happier. All four of my children inherited this love of unique tastes from me. We may have been out of milk, eggs, bread, and meat when they were growing up, but by golly we always had condiments aplenty. I remember one of the kids, as a teenager, opening the fridge and hollering something like, "Mom! What can I make for a snack with twenty kinds of mustard, a jar of pickle relish, mango chutney, and thirteen kinds of barbecue sauce?" Even today my motto is "It's all about the sauce." But I will admit the sauce tends to be tastier when there is something edible and solid beneath it.

When it comes to breakfast, however, I'm a One-Note Nelly. For a year I've munched the same breakfast between sips of coffee: a handful of almonds and a handful of dried cherries. I'm nonfunctional in the morning, and it takes every sleepy neuron I own just to make coffee, much less attempt such high-functioning feats as toasting a bagel or, God forbid, pouring a bowl of cereal. Still, when it comes to Same-Meal-Everyday wonders, I have to give the prize for OCD eating behaviors to my son-in-law, Rachel's husband, Jared. He gets enamored with one dish like nobody I've ever seen. He happily enjoys the same lunch every day: a peanut butter and honey sandwich. Never tires of it and never varies the formula. I am certain that if Jared lived in the day when God got on his most famous one-meal-wonder streak, serving a manna-only menu for years, my laidback son-in-law would have reacted only with gratitude and nary a complaint. He'd have sung a sincere blessing over his plain vanilla manna, freshly dropped from the heavens day after day. I, on the other hand, would be trying to spice it up in any way possible, with whatever herb, plant, or cacti I could scrounge up in the desert, a Jewish version of Bubba from *Forrest Gump*. Yenta Bubba. "Oy vey! You can barbecue it, broil it, or bake it! I got ya manna bagels, ya manna matzo ball soup, ya chopped livuh manna …"

Currently, Jared is on a two-year guacamole and tortilla chips streak. In fact, he gets a little nervous if there isn't a lineup of correctly ripening avocados on the kitchen counter: some ripe for today, a few that will be ripe tomorrow, and a couple that will ripen for the next day. A three-day supply gives him real peace of mind. Rachel has come to expect his daily call on the way home from work, asking, "Do you need me to get anything at the store? Milk? Bread? Avocados?"

"I thought I was supposed to be the one with the food cravings right now," Rachel said in a phone conversation when she was still newly pregnant, the baby now the size of an olive. "I'm just glad he's on to a new favorite food. Thank goodness he's finally off of the Roasted Corn Bean Salsa kick." She paused and sighed. "I swear our marriage could have come to a screeching halt over his daily bean salsa addiction."

I laughed aloud remembering one of the zaniest nights in our shared history together, when Rach and Jared had been married for almost three years. It was part *Keystone Cops*, part *I Love Lucy*, part *Iron Chef*, part *Emergency 911*. And it all started with Roasted Corn Bean Salsa.

Like a typical crime movie, we each had a different view of

what occurred that fateful night. It started out with our gathering for a week-long vacation in a two-bedroom condo in Galveston, Texas. Greg and I were tucked in bed; he was reading a book, and I was well on my way to dreamland. My parents were in another room also getting ready for their midsummer night's dream. Rachel and Jared were planning to sleep on the fold-out couch in the living room.

All I remember next was the sound of the smoke alarm piercing our respective ears at a pitch so sharp that I wondered if we'd ever hear normally again. I walked out of the bedroom and into the kitchen just in time to see Jared catapult over the back of the couch in a botched effort to reach the smoke alarm to turn it off. Though there was steam rising from the kitchen stove, it was nothing compared to the steam rising from Rachel's head. My mother, whom my kids call "Granny," had emerged in her robe at the sound of the alarm and was now doubled over in laughter. She finds humor wherever she can, and Jared's somersault was as fine a display of physical comedy as she'd seen since Dick Van Dyke tripped into his living room on America's black-and-white TVs in the early '60s.

My father sort of stumble-walked from their bedroom now, holding his ears, looking like a confused toddler. We all gathered in the kitchen to share the family bonding experience of being dazed and confused together, ears aching from the alarm's relentless scream, shouting questions we could not hear answers to, which only made Mom and I laugh harder and Rachel roll her eyes toward the ceiling with increased exasperation.

All of us were there, that is, except for Greg who remained calmly in bed, turning the pages in his book, his reading glasses perched on his nose, certain the unfortunate smoke and siren's blare would pass as quickly as it came. Where Mom and I found absolute hilarity (we were now both laughing so hard we were leaning on each other for support), and Rachel fought back supreme aggravation, Greg was the epitome of calm during chaos. Someone, I suppose, has to be the cool head that will prevail.

At this point, I'll let Rachel fill you in on the back story that led to the smoke alarm and brought us to this point in the unfolding saga.

RACHEL

About a month before we gathered in the Galveston condo, Jared and I had transitioned to a vegan diet, a change no one, not even the two of us, could have predicted. Though I've always been health conscious, my idea of a balanced diet was basically to maximize protein and minimize fat. I mostly cooked fish or chicken and relied on reduced fat cheese sticks and yogurt as the base of most of my snacks. I liked vegetables a lot, but they didn't play a leading role in my diet. They were mostly there to jazz up the entrée.

Then there is my husband, Jared, a Texan through and through: a barbecuin', huntin', fishin', baseball and football coachin', die-hard Longhorn fan. When we first met, he was one of the pickiest eaters I'd ever come across, refusing to eat onions, mushrooms, bell peppers, tomatoes, avocados, olives, mayonnaise, cream cheese, sour cream, bananas, a berry of any kind, chocolate, or even garlic. Who doesn't like garlic ... or chocolate?

When he ordered food at a restaurant he used phrases that were almost painful to hear: "dry," "with meat and cheese only," "plain vanilla," "no sauce or toppings." With Jared's ban on most things I considered tasty and delicious, I really didn't enjoy cooking much as a newlywed. After a couple years of catering to his boring taste buds, I couldn't take it anymore. I decided to try and win him over one prohibited ingredient at a time. I started with garlic, sneaking it into sauces or sautéing chicken in a garlic infused oil, only telling him the secret ingredient after he'd approved of the dish.

Before long, he announced I was free to cook with garlic. A small victory! Using this sneaky technique, I slowly expanded his food horizons and the "approved" ingredient list.

Almost three years into our marriage, on a road trip, Jared and I grabbed an audio book from the stack I'd grabbed in a hurry from our local library. It was a book on healthy eating, but we had no clue it would be about a diet free of all animal products. It debunked almost everything we knew about health:

- **Cow's milk:** good for baby cows, bad for humans
- **High-protein diets:** unbalanced and even harmful
- **Carbs and fat:** not all evil

Results from studies supporting this plant-based (or vegan) lifestyle were astounding: heart-disease reversed, diabetes cured, almost nonexistent rates of certain cancers. We were intrigued.

To my shock, Jared proposed we give it a try. When I questioned his aversion to vegetables and asked what he thought he would eat, he promised to try to eat everything I cooked for a month, without complaint. I was less enthusiastic about trying a vegan diet (which I doubted would last long) than I was about Jared's willingness to expand his eating horizons. I could hardly wait to get cooking!

As the Condiment Queen's daughter, I felt I had a new lease on my cooking life and hit the produce and spice aisles with unbridled enthusiasm. I thrived in this transition from eating animals to eating plants by reading vegan blogs, scouring the web for creative recipes, shopping natural groceries for new and intriguing ingredients, and cooking up exotic dishes like Vegetarian Spring Rolls with Garlic Ginger Sauce, Cauliflower and Kale Curry, and Seiten (sounds like say-ten) Stir Fry. Jared wasn't always enthusiastic about my culinary experiments, arguing that, "There may be a reason they named this recipe after Satan." But overall he was a good sport and kept his promise.

While "goin' vegan," I was having a blast discovering new recipes and foods to try. Jared, however, thrived in the comfort of familiarity. In the midst of so much change and my wild, adventurous cooking streak, he was soothed by repetition of a few new favorite dishes. Like any good Texan, he loves Mexican food, the spicier the better, which first led to his obsession with Corn Bean Salsa.

It started innocently enough as a simple recipe I made with a can of corn, a can of black beans, a few finely diced onions and bell peppers, jalapeños, cilantro, a squeeze of fresh lime, and a dash of salt and pepper. Jared liked it so much he asked me to make it again.

And again.

And again.

Until he came to expect his beloved Corn Bean Salsa would *always* be in the refrigerator. I was glad he liked it, but I eventually began to despise making it. This was my month to get creative and try a variety of new recipes. After a while, no matter how many variations of this salsa I made, it was starting to nauseate me. I just couldn't take it anymore!

Resentment began rearing its ugly little head, as Jared added it to every meal I made. I'd hand him a beautiful plate of baked falafel, homemade hummus, and Greek salad. He'd smother it with black beans and corn.

I'd serve a bowl of lentil spaghetti with garlic toast and kale chips, and he'd mix his prized salsa into the sauce. In exasperation I asked him, "Why am I even bothering to cook for you if all you really want is a can of beans and corn?"

To be fair, though Jared "seasoned" every dish I made with his salsa, he did eat what I put on his plate and ate it enthusiastically. Still I was up to my ears in corn, beans, and jalapeños, and I refused to enable Jared's salsa addiction any longer.

"From now on," I told him, "if you want Corn Bean Salsa, you'll have to make it yourself."

As any hardcore addict would do, Jared found a way to not only feed his addiction but take it to the next level. My simple version no longer cut it. He needed something stronger, so he started sautéing and roasting the veggies and adding more and more spice. His recipe was getting so spicy, I couldn't even eat it if I'd wanted to. He was cutting me out of the whole salsa deal, one jalapeño at a time.

Which brings me back to the fire alarm. By the time we arrived at the condo, Jared's evolved recipe called for him to sauté fresh jalapeños. Have you ever sautéed jalapeños? I don't recommend it. It involves a lot of coughing and crying and looking for an open window.

We didn't live far from the beach condo at the time, so we were planning on staying just one night with Mom and Greg and my grandparents. After everyone had gone to bed that evening, Jared hopped off of the fold-out couch where we had just settled in and started digging items out of his duffel bag. "I packed ingredients for corn bean salsa," he confessed with a sly grin. "Between you, your mom, and grandmother, I better take advantage of the open kitchen while I can."

"No, please don't," I begged. "We're in a 700-square-foot condo. The noise will wake up my family, the smell will linger, and the jalapeño steam piping through the vents might send my grandparents into cardiac arrest."

As addicts do, he insisted he had everything under control. He would be very quiet; he wouldn't harm anyone; he'd only cook the jalapeños a little. Frustrated and nervous, I sat up on our fold-out bed and mumbled under my breath as he chopped veggies, banged pans, and sautéed the dreaded jalapeño-veggie mixture. I coughed with extra gusto and dramatically wiped away tears from my stinging eyes. Without a stove vent in the condo kitchen, the air really was starting to thicken and a foggy haze filled the condo.

I could see that Jared was even starting to sweat nervously, so he began fanning the door to clear the air. And then it happened. The loudest, most ear-piercing sound cut through the thick air, and bright lights flashed through the fog. My family members started sleepily, stumbling from their rooms one at a time. I sat up in bed unable to speak or move.

He'd set off the fire alarm. Why wouldn't he just listen to me? Why couldn't he go one stinkin' day without that stupid salsa? "That's it," I silently determined, "he's starting a twelve-step program as soon as we get home!"

BECKY

I gained enough composure to open the front door to our third-floor condo, hoping to air out the smoke and haze, and what I saw was so unbelievable that I stood there for a second, mouth open, slack-jawed. The red light on every condo front porch was flashing and every single condo's smoke alarm was going off. Everyone in the entire complex was standing out front in their robes or T-shirts and sweat pants, rubbing their eyes, thinking the same thing: "What the heck?" There was no smoke, no fire, nobody seemed to think we were in any immediate danger, so nobody moved from their perch on their porches.

Off in the distance — and I am *not* making this up — I could see three fire trucks with lights flashing and sirens blaring, heading down the highway toward us.

Jared looked sheepish, but we were both thinking, "Seriously? One smoking jalapeño in one condo, and they are sending the entire Galveston fire department to put it out?"

Thankfully, before Jared confessed his bean-salsa crime, a lady below us said, "It's all my fault! I was just making popcorn in the microwave, and it burnt and the alarms went off ... and ... I'm so sorry!"

Such relief. Now everything made perfect sense. The entire city fire department was not coming to rescue the lot of us from Jared's smoking salsa: they were coming, en masse, to fire hose a bag of burnt popcorn.

Meanwhile, on the fold-out couch in the living room ...

RACHEL

Jared had not only managed to slip out of guilt, but had succeeded in leaving my mom and grandmother in stitches. He knows there's no better way to win them over than making them laugh. Here I was trying to prove how unthoughtful he'd been, and he had them giggling and hugging and—worst of all—clamoring for his recipe. (What's up with that? I'm supposed to be the funny foodie in this relationship!)

He crawled into the fold-out couch where I had positioned myself under the covers, my back turned toward him. He leaned over me, kissed my cheek, and whispered, "See, I told you that cooking the salsa wouldn't be a big deal. Good night, sweetie. I love you."

I guess I should be thankful that Jared doesn't get tired of the same old thing day in and day out—there's something to be said about a loyal man who always kisses me goodnight no matter what, trusting that eventually his wife will see the humor in his fiascos.

He was right. In spite of myself, I did laugh the next morning as Mom and Granny retold the story, enjoying the details all over again.

But don't tell Jared I told you that.

RECIPES THAT TEXANS GO OCD OVER
Jared's 15-Alarm (and 3-Fire-Truck) Roasted Corn Bean Salsa

After the fire-truck fiasco, Jared and I agreed to find a compromise between my simple recipe and his cough-inducing version. This one has a friendly level of heat, approved by friends and family. If you are a hardcore spice fanatic, feel free to add more jalapeños or throw in a serrano pepper for a real kick. —Rachel

Makes about 2 cups.

- 1 can black beans, rinsed, drained, and patted dry
- 1½ cups frozen corn (or 1 can, rinsed, drained, and patted dry)
- nonstick cooking spray (or olive oil)
- ½ of a red bell pepper (yields about ½ cup), diced to size of corn kernels
- ¼ cup of finely diced onion
- 2 jalapeños, seeded and finely diced (can use serranos for more spice or ½ a poblano pepper for less spice, or omit and use the other half of the red bell pepper for a mild version)
- ½ teaspoon seasoning salt
- ½ teaspoon cumin
- ½ teaspoon smoked paprika (or regular paprika)
- ¼ teaspoon salt
- 1 clove garlic, minced or very finely diced
- ½ cup loosely packed cilantro, chopped
- squeeze of lime juice to taste

Preheat oven to 400°. Spray a baking sheet with cooking spray or lightly oil. Put corn, bell peppers, onion, and jalapeño on the pan. Spray the veggies with cooking oil or very lightly coat with olive oil. Sprinkle on the spices and toss together. Put in oven for 15 minutes. Remove, add the garlic to the pan, stir, and put back in oven for 10 more minutes, stirring halfway. Remove and let cool. In a serving bowl, combine beans, corn mixture, cilantro, and a squeeze of lime juice to taste. Add a little more salt if desired. Chill and serve with chips. Will keep in the fridge for up to 2 days.

- • *Vegan/vegetarian*
- • *Gluten free*

White Bean Guacamole

By blending white beans into guacamole, it not only increases the protein and fiber and lowers the fat per serving, but it also stretches your buck when avocado prices are high. The pureed bean base gives the guacamole an extra creaminess too, but you'll never even know they're in there. —Rachel

Makes about 3 cups.

> 1 15-ounce can white beans (like cannellini or navy), drained with 1 tablespoon liquid reserved
>
> 2 avocados, halved and pitted
>
> 1 jalapeño pepper, seeded and chopped
>
> 1½ tablespoons lime juice
>
> 1 teaspoon salt
>
> ½ teaspoon pepper
>
> 1 teaspoon garlic powder
>
> 1 cup fresh cilantro

In a food processor, blend beans and reserved liquid until beans are pureed. Scoop the avocado flesh and chopped peppers into the food processor and pulse a few times. Add the lime juice, salt, pepper, garlic powder, and cilantro. Pulse until the desired consistency (I like a little bit of texture and a few chunks of avocado in mine). Serve with crackers or chips. I really like brown rice crackers even better than chips with this.

- • *Vegan/vegetarian*
- • *Gluten free*

Killer Chipotle and Roasted Pepper Salsa

This makes a lot, so I often freeze half to use at a later time. — *Becky*

Makes about a quart of salsa.

1 28-ounce can organic crushed fire-roasted tomatoes
  (divided in half)

½ red onion

2 garlic cloves, peeled

3 small mini peppers (yellow, orange, or red) or ½ large red
  pepper, roasted (Alternatives: if roasted hatch chilis are
  in season, these are delicious replacements or additions!
  Or you can use a couple of roasted peppers from a jar,
  small can green chilies, or roast some tomatillos.)

½ cup of cilantro

2 large fresh jalapeños, seeded

2 chipotle peppers in adobe sauce

2 tablespoons white vinegar

2 teaspoons sugar

sea salt to taste

½ fresh lime, squeezed

1 teaspoon smoked paprika (this just adds to the smokiness,
  but is not essential)

Put half of the crushed tomatoes and remaining ingredients in a
food processor. Pulse until mixture has the consistency you like
for salsa. Then stir in the rest of the crushed tomatoes, which will
give it a nice chunky texture. Check seasonings once more. Grab
a bag of chips, a margarita, and enjoy.

• Vegan/vegetarian
• Gluten free

Chapter 4

Shower the People We Love with … Lots of Showers

Pull up a chair. Take a taste. Come join us.
Life is so endlessly delicious.
Ruth Reichl

RACHEL

Shortly after our fire truck fiasco, Jared and I were in Gruene, Texas, a charming old town set along a sparkling river. We were enjoying the afternoon break during a marriage retreat for sports coaches and their wives. I had just eaten a basket full of the best French fries of my life at Mozie's Bar & Grill, just across from the oldest dance hall in Texas. Some foods leave a taste memory even years later, and these fries were in that category: long thin potato sticks, doused with fresh minced garlic and a generous seasoning of kosher salt, floating in a bath of butter or oil, or maybe both. (I was newly vegan and frequently employed the "don't ask, don't tell" rule in those early days, especially when it came to butter.) New coaching friends from the retreat joined us for lunch, and afterward we all walked to a winery, where we sampled and sipped on local merlots and pinot noirs while sitting around a rustic barrel table under the shade of sweeping oaks.

We experienced this weekend with a hundred other couples who were all familiar with "the coaching life." It proved a godsend to us. We'd just spent a year living near Galveston, where Jared coached high school baseball and football, both of us feeling a little lost and isolated from all that was familiar—friends, family, a church home. I was growing disillusioned with the company I'd started to help authors promote their books. During Mom and Greg's visit to the Texas coast, she and I had spent some time by their condo pool, day dreaming and brainstorming about possibilities of writing together. I felt God stirring my heart, readying it for big changes ahead.

Then the week before this retreat, Jared was offered a job in his hometown, just east of Dallas. We were thrilled. Not only would we move near lots of family, but with this ideal location, we decided to shop for our first home and finally put down some roots. Life was looking up. I'm not sure whether it was the good news, the garlic fries, or the wine, but my heart was full of hope and dreams for the first time in months.

I walked into a little country store, and my eyes drifted to a corner filled with pastel pinks and blues, bunny frames, and snuggly blankets. I picked up a book called *I'll Always Be Your Daughter*, a fable of a mother and daughter tree and the love that exists between them, even as she grows into a unique tree of her own, producing her own little acorn.[3] Jared and I had started talking about having a baby. At that moment, buoyed by joy, companionship, wine, and fries, I allowed myself to dream of the day when I could tell my mom, "I'm going to be a mother too," and this book seemed the perfect way to let her know. I purchased the slim volume and tucked it away to give to her someday ... when the time was right.

BECKY

I got that wonderful call from Rachel, confirming my dream that she was, indeed, pregnant just three months after she and Jared moved into their new home near Dallas.

As weeks turned into months, it was becoming clear that Rachel would be one of those adorable little pregnant women who only gets pregnant in the general vicinity of her belly. She looked more beautiful than I'd ever seen her, and that is saying a lot because my daughter has always been a head turner. I, on the other hand, was the sort of woman who seemed to get pregnant in every part of my body. During all of my pregnancies, I looked like I was carrying triplets: one baby in my belly and one tucked into each thigh.

By the start of my second trimester, I had been wearing maternity clothes for at least a month, and had a Paul Bunyan–sized appetite. I would no sooner finish off a stack of dinner plate–sized flapjacks for breakfast than I'd start dreaming about a Big Mac or two for lunch. Not only did food suddenly taste amazing, and not only did I eat it by the wheelbarrow full, but I had constant cravings for something exceedingly salty and vinegary. I tried pickles, chips, Italian dressing—and combinations thereof—but nothing exactly hit the spot. Until one day, I mixed up some grated Parmesan cheese (the kind in a green can, the only kind I knew existed in my twenties) with an equal amount of Worcestershire sauce and took a big bite of the gritty-brown concoction. Eureka! Craving satisfied. I would get near panicky when either the Parm or the Worcestershire started getting low, so I bought in bulk.

Thanks to the All Day–All Night Nursing Your Baby Diet, however, I would lose my pregnancy weight in no time. I went from looking like a walking Jell-O mold, to svelte and sporting a belt around a tiny waist again in less than four months. Besides the fact that a nursing baby takes an average of 800 calories a day out of your body, the babies themselves turn into personal trainers as soon as they can crawl. "Mini Bob Harpers," my sister calls them.

You might think from my aforementioned flapjack, Big Mac, Parmesan cheese, and Worcestershire cravings that I didn't think much about health in the early '80s. But you'd be wrong. The health guru of that era was Adelle Davis, and I read her books with Earth Mother fervency. So to supplement pancakes and burgers

I would make sure I also ate my fruits and veggies, got plenty of fresh milk (dairy was still tolerated by most of the planet), and drank nasty-tasting Brewer's yeast concoctions. I would liberally sprinkle toasted wheat germ on everything and clearly remember having a bowl of Blue Bell Chocolate Almond Marshmallow ice cream smothered in wheat germ right after I started labor with my second born son. All my babies weighed nearly 9 pounds, with my last-born son, Gabe, tipping the scale (literally—he almost fell off it) at 10 pounds 2 ounces. I'd like to mention that my children all had perfect Apgar scores at birth, which I've suggested they list alongside their grade points on job résumés.

Though, at an intellectual level, I trusted my daughter to design a healthy vegan pregnancy diet, I have to say there were times I wondered if her baby was getting enough nutrition. Since Rachel was gaining so little weight and her tummy was staying flat for so long, in my mind's eye I imagined her child to be an itsy-bitsy baby girl who might only grow to be the size of Thumbelina. She'd wear doll clothes and we could take her everywhere in our pockets. Her bed would be a candy dish with a hanky-size blankey—but no matter, we'd love her silly.

RACHEL

Every pregnant woman dreams of having a baby shower, and I was no exception. As soon as we returned from our twentieth-week sonogram, we announced that the shopping for all things baby *boy* could begin. With Jared's big family, my dad's family, and my mother and her family all excited about welcoming the new grandson, I ended up, all in all, having *four* celebrations. At times the back-to-back showers felt more like a deluge.

My mom's sister, Aunt Rachel, for whom I'm named, gave me a shower I like to refer to as "The Arnold Baby Shower, Game Show, and Musical Revue."

After we'd enjoyed cake, played a game, and opened baby gifts, my Broadway lovin' Aunt Rachel arranged chairs, audience style, at the bottom of the stairs and asked us to have a seat. Then she hit a button on a boom box. Her eleven-year-old daughter, my cousin Tori, came pirouetting down the stairs in her yellow ballerina tutu, ending her performance with a dramatic en pointe twirl. Then the music shifted dramatically to a hip-hop beat and out bounced grinning, dimpled Whitney, Tori's little sister, in her splatter-paint tights, lime-green shorts, and black-and-electric-pink T-shirt, performing a jazz routine with moves as big as her personality. Unorthodox as this ending to a baby shower may have been, Mom's side of the family believes any occasion, however casual, can be improved and livened up by the addition of show tunes, impromptu comedy, costumes, or dancing.

~

Bless her heart, Michelle, my best friend since we were three years old, was an unsuspecting victim of my unquenchable need for control. With all the uncertainties involved in pregnancy, I desperately wanted to feel in control of one thing I knew I could do and do well: organize one of the many upcoming baby showers. So I manipulated a takeover of sorts. Michelle had a full schedule of classes and a young daughter, and after begging her for the twelfth time to let me help, she handed me the reins on the menu, much to the delight of my inner control freak. Gone was her simple menu involving finger sandwiches, chips, and a preordered cake. In its place I created an elaborate all-vegan, all-homemade menu. The night before the shower, Michelle and her precocious three-year-old daughter, Avery, came with their overnight bags packed, ready to prep the food and prepare for the shower even if it took all night. Which it almost did.

We chopped colorful veggies, adding them to tri-colored cooked pasta, olives, chickpeas, and Italian dressing for a tangy

cold salad. We made baggies of sliced strawberries, sliced manda-
rin oranges, and slivered almonds to pile onto baby spinach and
drizzle with poppy seed dressing the next day. In a nod to my
strangest pregnancy craving, we spread whole wheat tortillas with
buffalo vegan cream cheese and wrapped them around dill pickles,
then sliced them into pinwheels. I made homemade ranch dressing for dipping veggies, but it turned out bland and runny, like
something from a Dark Hidden Valley. I've since perfected the
recipe and am happy to report it is rich and creamy and beats any
bottled dressing I've ever had, but flat-spoken little Avery took
one taste of that batch, put one hand on her tiny hip and declared,
"That ain't ranch dressin'." Working into the wee hours of the
night, Michelle and I put the "icing on the cake," à la homemade
agave cupcakes with vanilla icing. They turned out moist and sub-
tly sweet and would be the hit of the party. I let Avery test-taste
one before the event, and she was the first of many to declare them
"the best cupcakes ever." The whole affair was a huge success.

~

To say Jared's family are Texas Longhorn fans would be like saying that my mom is a tiny bit disorganized. They are also the most
avid sports parents you've ever seen. This love of games extends
everywhere: at the Randolph shower we played — and I'm not
making this up — *seven* baby-themed games. At the end of it we'd
all worked up an impressively athletic sweat. My shower from the
Randolphs was a whirlwind of burnt orange onesies, Longhorn
pacifiers, fuzzy stuffed footballs, and sports-themed outfits. I
realized it was a very real possibility that our child's first sentence
might be, "Hook 'em Horns."

But the most treasured surprise was from Jared's mom,
Rhonda. It was a small blue romper with a white collared shirt, a
white newsboy hat, and matching Keds, well-worn by my husband
when he was a little boy. This loving gift from my mother-in-law

felt like the passing of the torch, a symbol of how intertwined our lives were truly becoming now that I was carrying her son's child.

BECKY

Knowing Rachel would be thoroughly showered (or "doused") in the traditional way, I began to visualize a more unique style of welcoming the new grandbaby—one that would be more *Under the Tuscan Sun* than *Under the Sea*. More Michael Bublé than Brahms's lullabies.

Call me a party pooper, but my idea of a rousing good time has never involved a room full of bright, mature women playing Pin the Diaper on the Baby or counting out sheets of toilet paper to guess the girth of a pregnant mother. Just thinking about sipping Sprite and sherbet punch alongside a store-bought cake with frosting made of powdered sugar, Crisco, and food dye made my teeth ache.

So I dreamed up a "Girls' Night Out Mediterranean Dinner Party-Shower" idea. Rachel loved it. Either that or she was too wiped out from hormones or the nonstop shower planning in Texas to have strong opinions anymore. I sent invitations saying, "Come help us welcome Rachel's Baby Boy with a dinner party and conversation! (No party games and lots of wine!) Woot! Woot!" Then I booked a flight out of Dallas for Rachel, and two more flights out of Seattle for my daughter-in-law, Julie, and four-year-old Georgie, both of whom adore Rachel, babies, and any excuse for a party.

In the days before the shower, I dove into the kitchen feeling like Mario Batali on a mission to feed Italy and the Greek Isles. I made a vegetarian lasagna, a meaty moussaka, a big Greek salad, and an elegant Italian crème cake. (Though I gave in and decorated it with colorful pacifiers and baby spoons.) Julie created a stunning tray of fresh strawberries dipped and drizzled in dark and white chocolate. (Georgie "helped" by sampling the results. With his mouth, cheeks, and chin smudged with chocolate, he declared them "not poisonous.") We served vegan-friendly Italian sodas for the pregnant and nursing moms, made of Italian sparkling water, fruit juice, and a dash of coconut cream. Stressed-out mothers of toddlers and teens, along with grandmas and empty nesters, were given crystal glasses of good wine. It was early spring, so I purchased a rainbow of hydrangeas in pretty pots to double as decorations and party favors, alongside vases of vibrant purple, orange, and yellow Gerber daisies.

Guests filed in with beautiful gift bags and those genuine smiles women have on their faces when they are about to enjoy a night off from childcare and cooking. There were several women from our church who, over the years of celebrations and crises, became like bonus daughters to me and extra sisters to Rachel. Several of my peers (most of them writers) who have come to know and love Rachel from her visits and through Facebook, arrived, adding to the fun and chick-chat, along with the family already assembled.

RACHEL

The main memory I have of my Colorado shower is laughter. Without a single party game, we gals found a way to entertain each other and laughed the whole evening — over dinner, dessert, and while opening presents — many times to the point of side aches and tears.

I also remember being moved by the thoughtfulness of these friends from afar. There were several homemade gifts, including a hand-sewn colorful bohemian style "wet bag" (to hold cloth diapers), an up-cycled baby T-shirt appliquéd with a wild black-and-green polka-dot man's tie, and a chubby hand-crocheted penguin.

Later that night, my little nephew George inspected all of the gifts with great interest. I read him some of the new baby's books; and then he picked up the stuffed penguin and held it to my belly, making it dance and squeak, to "show" to his baby cousin. George loves babies more than any other little boy I've known. At church that weekend, he immediately spotted all the babies in mothers' arms and nudged his Nonny (my mom) toward them. He would silently walk over to each one, gaze in their eyes, and touch their heads as if giving a blessing. Then he'd move on to the next baby and do the same. In an uncanny way he understood that there was a real live child inside me. Frequently he would stop whatever little-boy activity he was doing and come find me standing in the kitchen or sitting on the couch. He would gently reach up and place his little hand on my belly and just hold it there, without saying a word. Then off he'd go to dive off the steps again or to grab another bite of an apple.

After I opened all of my gifts, and most of the girls were sipping their second glass of wine, I handed my mom a gift bag containing a token of my appreciation for the shower. She opened it, then stood up to shout with joy, and immediately wrapped it around her waist to show off. "You know how much I've been coveting this! Thank you!" Then she struck a glamour pose, hand behind her head asking, "How do I look?"

Well, she looked as beautiful and nerdy as any woman can look wearing a baby-blue fanny pack roughly the size of a flattened basketball.

The women in the room were laughing and curious. "Okay, what's the story with this, Rachel?" one friend asked.

"Well, Mom has always loved fanny packs in that way only quirky people can," I answered.

"They are so practical!" Mom said, defending herself. "Like a hands-free purse. And I can't misplace it!"

I leaned back in the rocker, patted my belly, and warmed to my story. "So, a few years ago, when Jared worked for a Catholic private school, they had a big fancy dinner-auction to raise money. We perused the items and saw that a basket of spa goodies was getting bids high enough to pay our rent. We were in way over our financial heads. And that is when I spied it, The Mother of All Fanny Packs. It was huge and sported not only two pockets but a water bottle, a padded belt, and reflective gear. While Jared was glad-handing the booster club, I sneaked away to offer a $5.00 bid on the fanny pack, under his name."

"You are so bad," Mom said, then quickly added, "I love that about you."

"So at the end of the evening," I continued," I asked Jared if he thought we might have won anything. He reminded me that we hadn't placed any bids. 'Well,' I said, 'I think I saw your name on one of the items.' He looked at me warily and said, 'Rachel ... what did you buy?' 'Don't worry,' I told him, 'You are going to *love* it. And it only cost us $5.00!' Jared looked relieved, impressed, and curious."

"So then," I continued with a wicked little grin, "I led Jared to the table with the monster fanny pack, pointed to it, and without cracking a smile said, 'Don't you love it?' His eyes widened and he whispered, "No way am I going to carry that thing out of here." So I confidently clipped it around my evening dress. I knew Mom would have been so proud of me."

"And I am," Mom said, nodding.

"Anyway, I posted a picture of me in my pretty dress and industrial-size fanny pack on Facebook. It got some good laughs. Then, awhile later, a comment from Mom popped up asking me if I was still using the fanny pack, saying she'd been looking for one to hold her portable CD player when she went for walks. 'Are you asking for our prized fanny pack?' I teased her. 'First, I'll have to see if Jared is willing to part with it.' Of course, Jared could not wrap it up and put it in my suitcase fast enough."

As the laughter settled down, I said, "Mom, there's one more gift in the bag."

She reached in and took out the book I had been holding on to for ten months, waiting for the right news and then the right moment. Sitting down with the fanny pack still wrapped around her waist, she opened the book and began reading *I'll Always Be Your Daughter: A Fable for Mothers and Daughters.*

BECKY

I fought back the lump in my throat as I read the simple story of a mama tree and her little acorn "daughter" ... how the acorn dropped from the tree's branch, but a squirrel carried it out of the mama tree's reach. The daughter tree reassures the mother that "it is warmer when I am not in your shadow." That she can grow better, and, even though they are in separate distinct places, "I will still be your Daughter."

I thought of how hard it has been to be so far from Rachel, with her living in Texas and me in Colorado, and how much harder it might be once my grandson arrived. Yet, despite the miles, we've managed to see each other often and stay as close as any mother and daughter could hope for.

Then, in the storybook fable, a drought comes and the Mother and Daughter trees are parched with thirst. "I can bear it for myself," cried the Mother, "but not for my Daughter." The Mother sets about praying for rain. As I read, I remembered the pain I'd endured in my own life, and then the double dose of pain I experienced during a season of pain in Rachel's life, when she suffered a similar blow to the heart. When the rain did not come in answer to the Mama Tree's prayers, she despaired. But the Daughter Tree soothed her mother's worry by assuring her that tough times would make her roots grow deeper. "And yes, Mother, even though you cannot change the world for me, I will still be your daughter."

And on the fable goes, as the Mother learns that she can't

protect her daughter from hurt and struggle, that her daughter loves her always, has in fact grown into a woman and a friend, but will sing her own songs, create her own shade, and "produce her own acorn." A little acorn that will draw love and strength and life from her—but will also grow up and find his or her own unique place in the sun.

And then this Mama Tree smiled clear down to her roots—and adjusting the fanny pack around her trunk, hugged her independent and loving Daughter Tree and her Little Acorn within.

There were happy tears.

And it was good.

RECIPES FOR AN ITALIAN FEAST
Becky's Layered Italian Veggie Casserole

A slice of Italian veggie heaven. This is a wonderful healthy casserole to make at the beginning of the week, then slice and re-heat for lunches or side dishes. —*Becky*

Serves 10 to 12.

   1–3 tablespoons olive oil

   1 eggplant, peeled, sliced into ¼ inch rounds (If you don't like eggplant, you can substitute 3 portobello mushrooms, sliced, instead)

   2 small or 1 large potato, unpeeled, sliced into ¼ inch rounds

   ⅓ cup water

   4 cups marinara sauce

   6 slices or 1 cup grated Swiss or Gruyère cheese

   4 zucchini squash, sliced into ¼ inch rounds

   4 yellow squash, sliced into ¼ inch rounds

   ⅔ cup grated Parmesan

   2 tablespoons olive oil

   2 tablespoons butter

1½ cups crushed buttery whole wheat crackers

1 teaspoon oregano or Italian seasoning

salt and pepper

Preheat oven to 350°. In large skillet, pour enough olive oil to coat the bottom of the skillet. Heat to medium high. Sauté eggplant slices for about a minute per side or until partially cooked. Using tongs, place eggplant in a layer in bottom of 11x13 inch baking dish. Partially cook potato in same skillet, adding ⅓ cup water. Then add this layer on top of the eggplant. Lightly salt and pepper the eggplant-potato layer. Pour 2 cups marinara sauce on top of potato and eggplant. Lay Swiss cheese on top of this layer. Next (using same skillet), lightly sauté zucchini and yellow squash together, adding more oil if needed. Put this layer on top of Swiss cheese. Lightly salt and pepper the squash. Pour 2 more cups of marina on top of squash. Sprinkle with Parmesan cheese. Melt butter with olive oil in skillet, add crushed crackers, and stir until evenly coated. Pour buttered crackers atop casserole. Sprinkle with oregano or Italian seasoning. Bake at 350° until cheese is hot and melted and crackers are golden brown, about 20 to 30 minutes.

• *Vegetarian*

Sundried Tomato and Artichoke Bowtie Pasta

Without any pasta sauce on hand, I added some white cooking wine and the flavorful herb-packed oil from my jar of sundried tomatoes to a simple pasta with diced veggies, sundried tomatoes, artichokes, and gently wilted spinach. This is so pretty and flavorful. It makes a stunning centerpiece at the table. Top with roasted chickpeas (see Puttanesca Sauce recipe in Chapter 1) or vegan sausage to make it a complete one-dish meal. —Rachel

Serves 4.

16 ounces whole wheat bowtie pasta

1 can quartered artichoke hearts

1 6-ounce jar sundried tomatoes packed in olive oil
    and herbs

1 tablespoon olive oil

1 small onion, chopped

1 zucchini, chopped

1 yellow squash, chopped

2 cloves of garlic, minced

2 cups fresh spinach

3 tablespoons white cooking wine

salt and pepper to taste

2 tablespoons chopped parsley (optional)

While prepping the veggies, boil the water and cook the pasta
as directed on the box. If the sundried tomatoes are whole, chop
them up, reserving the oil in the jar. In a large pan, heat about a
tablespoon of olive oil on medium heat; add onions and a sprinkle
of salt. Sauté for 2–3 minutes. Add zucchini, squash, and sauté
for about 3 more minutes. Add the garlic and a touch more oil
if needed. Sauté until garlic is translucent. Add artichokes, sundried tomatoes, spinach, and white cooking wine and sauté until
spinach is just wilted. Gently toss the drained pasta in with the
veggies. Pour in just enough of the oil and herbs from the sundried
tomatoes to lightly coat everything. Season with salt and pepper
to taste and garnish with fresh chopped parsley.

- Vegan/vegetarian
- Gluten-free friendly (substitute gluten-free pasta, like the ones
  made of quinoa, corn, or rice)

Rustic Sausage and Peppers Skillet

*My first real job was as a hostess at an Italian restaurant with an
open kitchen. From my hostess stand, I could see the chefs tossing
pizzas into the wood oven and dropping pasta into boiling water.*

This recipe was inspired by a hot skillet dish they served. You always knew when someone ordered it because a cloud of smoke would plume into the air as they poured the sauce into the piping hot pan. The cloud followed the waiter all the way to the table, making a dramatic presentation for our guests. Though I've toned down the smoke and mirrors here, the flavor is just as exciting as I remember theirs to be more than a decade ago. —Rachel

Serves 2.

- ½ package of whole wheat spaghetti, cooked al dente (1 minute less than recommended cooking time)
- 2 tablespoons olive oil
- 1 onion, sliced in thin strips
- 1 green bell pepper, sliced in strips
- 2 links of Smoked Apple Sage Field Roast Sausages, sliced into ½ inch rounds
- 2–3 cloves of garlic, sliced into thin "chips"
- 2 cups of spicy pasta sauce such as arrabiata or spicy marinara (my recipe for arrabiata sauce is available on our blog)

Generously coat a large skillet (iron or stainless steel work better than a nonstick for this recipe) with olive oil, and heat on medium heat. When warm, add onions and sauté for a few minutes until they start to get soft. Add bell peppers and sausage, and turn to almost medium-high heat. Stir every minute or so until the onions, bell peppers, and sausage are slightly charred. Turn off heat. Stir in garlic chips for a couple of minutes until translucent, being careful not to let them burn. Stir in al dente pasta and pasta sauce. Turn heat back on to low and heat until warmed through. Serve immediately.

- Vegan/vegetarian
- Gluten free (Field Roast is made with wheat gluten, so substitute chickpeas — or a cooked sweet Italian sausage if you eat meat — and gluten-free pasta, like the ones made of quinoa, corn, or rice)

Pesto Parmesan Chicken

This is the best Chicken Parmesan I've made; better yet, the prettiest Chicken Parmagiano I've ever seen. The chicken inside stays incredibly tender, and when you cut through it, you can see the pretty layer of green pesto, golden panko, red marinara, and white cheese. Now that's amore! It's excellent served with a side of angel-hair pasta that has been tossed in a little extra pesto. —Becky

Serves 2 people (with big appetites).

    2 large boneless chicken breasts
    salt and pepper (to taste, to sprinkle lightly on chicken)
    2 cups marinara sauce (your favorite bottled brand or
        homemade; my recipe for quick marina is available
        on our blog)
    ¼ cup fresh or grated mozzarella
    ¼ cup olive oil
    1 tablespoon butter
    ½ cup pesto
    1 cup panko breadcrumbs
    1 cup grated Parmesan cheese, divided

Preheat oven to 400°. Heat the marina in a saucepan until hot. Put olive oil and butter in a large ovenproof skillet (such as cast iron or stainless steel) and heat to medium high.

Rinse and pat boneless chicken breasts dry. Sprinkle both sides lightly with salt and pepper. Put pesto in a shallow bowl. In another shallow bowl mix panko and ½ cup Parmesan cheese. Lay chicken breasts, one at a time, into pesto first, coating both sides of breast and edges thoroughly, and then in panko-Parmesan mixture, coating both sides and edges of breasts thoroughly again.

Sauté the breasts in the oil and butter on both sides until the coating is crispy and golden. You may have to add a little more oil depending on size of breasts and your pan. (Drain off excess oil, if there is a lot of it, before putting in oven.)

Then put the entire skillet into the oven and cook for about 5 minutes. Remove from oven and ladle each breast with ¼ cup marinara, 2 tablespoons mozzarella, and 2 tablespoons Parmesan cheese. Place back in the oven for 5 to 10 more minutes or until cheese is melted and chicken breasts are cooked, but not overly so. (A meat thermometer is helpful here — thickest part of chicken should be 160° – 165° — but if you don't have one, just cut through the middle of one of the breasts to check for doneness.) Before serving, ladle each breast with more marinara and sprinkle with more Parmesan cheese.

Quick Method: Use thinner chicken breasts or pound smaller chicken breasts thin. Put sauce and cheese on immediately after pan frying, and cook in oven only until cheese melts.

Chapter 5

Stocking Up, Nesting, and Losing Control

> *I like a cook who smiles out loud*
> *when he tastes his own work.*
> *Let God worry about your modesty;*
> *I want to see your enthusiasm.*
> Robert Farrar Capon

RACHEL

At my thirty-six-weeks-of-gestation appointment (bigger than a honeydew, smaller than a pumpkin), my midwife said, "I am predicting you won't make it to your due date."

Part of me was relieved because I just couldn't see how my skin could stretch any more. I already felt beyond capacity. My once-trim ankles had swollen into "cankles." And my breasts, good grief, they seemed to have taken on a life of their own. I'd officially entered "Eat Your Heart Out, Dolly Parton" territory.

The day before my appointment, I'd waddled myself into Babies-R-Us to buy a nursing bra, grabbing a few options in what I thought was my size, then wandered around the store looking for the dressing room. An associate said, "I'm sorry there are no dressing rooms, but there is a Mother's Room on the other side of the store that you can use." I found the room and looked around. There was a rocking chair, a changing table, and a cushy bench. *Cozy,* I thought. I put the bras on the bench, and reached to lock the door. There was no lock, but I peeked out and saw on the outside of the door a post-it-note sized sign that read Please Knock

Before Entering. *Oh well*, I thought, *what's the worst that could happen? A mother and her hungry baby barge in?*

I was wearing a summer dress, one of the few outfits I could still comfortably squeeze into, and realized the whole dress had to come off in order to try the bras on. Great. Some mom is going to get more than she bargained for if she doesn't pay attention to that itty bitty post-it-note.

My first round of attempts was eye opening. My cups over-flowed. In fact, these bra cups looked about the size of that post-it note on my ever-expanding body. I waddled back to the other side of the store, grudgingly grabbing some DDs, and waddled back. Tears filled my eyes as I realized I would need an E, an E! For Enormous! Who knew size E even existed? Let me tell you something: Victoria kept that a secret from me.

Back in the Mother's Room, exhausted and tearful, eight months pregnant and wearing nothing but my maternity granny panties, I stood there and held up the huge contraption, staring in disbelief. It looked like two ugly, plain beige bowling ball covers, stitched together. It was all I could do not to sob.

And then, during what I felt sure was my most sad and humbling pregnant moment, in walked a young man, no older than twenty, holding a bottle of disinfectant in one hand and paper towels in the other.

When he saw me in all my topless pregnant glory, he was stricken with instant paralysis. He just stood there, slack jawed, eyes wide. In a moment that felt like eternity, I watched this poor mortified boy soak in what would happen to his girlfriend if he ever knocked her up. It was probably the best lesson in celibacy he would ever encounter.

In a fluster, I grabbed my dress and tried to cover myself while blubbering, "Close the door! The sign says knock!" He didn't even blink, his eyes literally stuck like a deer in Size E headlights. He did, however, manage to mutter over and over, "I'm sorry. I'm so sorry."

"The door! Close it. Please!" I pleaded. Then added, "But leave first!"

Mercifully, his brain finally connected with his body, and he turned and walked out, closing the door and still muttering, "I'm so sorry."

I glanced in the mirror and tried to accept my new reality. The girls had gone wild.

~

Not only was my body out of control, but lately, I felt as though I were losing control of simple brain function. Decisions paralyzed me.

Normally, I'm all about the Boy Scout Motto, "Be Prepared." But four weeks before the Big Day, I hadn't washed a single onesie or even bought a car seat. Newly motivated by the midwife's prediction of an early labor, I got my pregnant self into gear, crossing off items on my task list with renewed gusto every day. Waddling as fast as I could, I painted the nursery, set up the crib, took inventory of gifts, ordered remaining essentials, made several trips to the big-box baby store, installed the car seat, and washed, folded, admired, and put away adorable pint-sized clothes in soft shades of blue and green. And I did this mostly on my own as Jared coached and traveled with a summer-league baseball team.

Once the nursery was set up, I was not quite ready to come down from my nesting high. So I turned my focus to the kitchen, preparing and freezing meals for the weeks following the birth. I roasted a purple eggplant, then chopped it up, mixing the fragrant cubes with crumbled tempeh and caramelized onions. Finally I simmered it all in a spicy tomato sauce and seasoned with a hint of licoricey fennel seeds, turning it into a rich, Greek-style filling. Then I portioned this luscious mixture into small pie tins and topped them with a rustic homemade biscuit dough. When I pulled the eight individual pies out of the oven, their bumpy mountain-top crusts steaming with goodness, I was filled with deep satisfaction.

A side of mashed potatoes would be nice with these, I thought. So I reached for some russets, and began chopping, boiling, and mashing them with vegan butter and almond milk. I was so proud of the yumminess coming out of my kitchen that I grabbed my chef's knife and began peeling back the layers of an onion. Before I knew it, the *mirepoix* (diced onions, celery, and carrots) was sizzling in olive oil. Soon lentils and diced tomatoes joined the party. I lined an empty spaghetti-sauce jar with quart-sized baggies, one on top of another, then filled each baggie, removed and sealed it, one after another. "Lentil Veggie Chili," I wrote on the bag, with instructions to "Defrost, reheat, serve with cornbread." *Cornbread ... hmm ... might as well whip up that recipe for vegan jalapeño cornbread I've been wanting to try.*

And on it went. I couldn't turn off my culinary burst of energy. I just wanted to cook and cook and cook.

I know a part of my cooking spree was to keep my mind and hands busy when all I had left to do was wait for labor to begin. When life makes *you* the watched pot, I say, throw in some sweet potatoes and make a breakfast casserole. Which I did, smiling as I watched the maple-pecan crumble topping caramelize under the broiler. I went on like this for days, freezing recipe after recipe. Waffles and hummus and muffins and soups and enchiladas and lentil-loafs and cookies and coconut covered cherries. My freezer was so full I had to remove the ice basket.

By the time I finally wound down, hung up my apron, and patted my bulging belly, I'd prepared more than twenty recipes.

A few days shy of my due date, I looked down at my Master Task List, smiled, and sighed. My tasks were almost complete. My house was spotless all the way down to the baseboards. (My midwife suggested I clean them as a way to help the baby's head settle into the correct position.) The nursery was finished. And my freezer was so full that there was danger of a food avalanche when I opened the door. All that was left was to simply give birth.

Piece. O'. Cake.

BECKY

The phone rang and I pounced on it, cat-on-mouse style, as I'd been doing for two weeks.

"Rachel? Is that you? Are you in labor?"

Rachel was only days from her due date. Though she is, as we've discussed, a natural "organizational genius," pregnancy can turn all of us into beings whom even we ourselves do not recognize.

In Rachel's well-ordered Birth Plan, the subsection entitled "When and How and How Long Mama Will Come to Help with the Baby" had not yet been filled out. Though this made me a little nervous, I told myself that this was because in Rachel's current state, her brain refused to make another decision. Months of researching the perfect cloth diapers (organic, cotton, soft, cute) and baby strollers (chic, expensive, or will double as a washing machine and a blender) had rendered her incapable of making any more choices. Her bedroom walls looked as though a toddler had been let loose with ten paint cans and a sponge, streaked with different paint samples and left that way—silently mocking her inability to choose anything, even a paint color.

I understood this and, as a woman who has coauthored three books with brain experts, I explained it to her. "The decision-making portion of your brain has now been sucked into your womb to help support the rest of your vital organs in the project of growing a baby. It may or may not migrate back to your head, and I cannot guarantee how long it will take if it does." (It is a scientific fact, which every mother can confirm, that every child takes a big tippy-sized cup of their mother's neurons during their formation and birth.)

By her ninth month of pregnancy, being asked by the clerk at the grocery store to choose between "paper or plastic?" could cause Rachel to break down in tears. As it turned out, the "Mom Coming to Help Out with Baby" part of her Birth Plan had two words scrawled under it: *Wing it.* After all, she knew if there was one thing she could count on about her mother, it is my ability to go with the flow.

Here were the complications involved: If Greg and I flew in, last minute, from Denver to Dallas, the airfares would be through the roof. If we drove the twelve hours, we might miss the baby's birth. If we arrived a few days ahead of time, Rachel would feel like a watched pot waiting to boil. Neither of us had a clear "next right step" in mind, so we just decided to do what felt best when the time came.

Apparently, that time had now come. Back to the phone call at hand.

"Well," Rachel's surprisingly calm voice said, "the midwife believes I could go into labor anytime now. I lost 'the plug,' as they say."

"So now the baby can slip down the drain at any moment?" I asked.

"Yep, that's basically the idea."

"Do you want us to start driving to Texas?"

"I don't know," Rachel said with a conflicted sigh. "I want you close by ... and I want you here for *sure* when the baby is born and when we come home from the hospital. But Jared and I really want to be home alone to labor quietly together as long as we can before we go to the hospital."

"I understand this desire for privacy," I said. "I really do." Then scenes of my four labors flashed in my memory. Back in my Earth Mother days (think Dharma of *Dharma and Greg*) my home births seemed more like casual parties, involving my mom in the kitchen, making sure there were yummy snacks and fresh drinks, a variety of our family members milling around, our kids (until a grandma or aunt took them "out to play" before any serious pain began), an occasional friend dropping by, and of course, the midwives chatting in various rooms in the house. When things got serious and I needed to push, the crowd thinned to give me more privacy for the main event. (Even so I did end up with several sweet pictures from my first son's birth, taken by a well-meaning relative, along with a few horrifying pictures of my nether regions I am still trying to erase from memory.) My mom still laughs about giving my freshly born son his first bath in the kitchen sink and having to move aside a huge sack of garden-fresh zucchini and a bowl of placenta to clear space for the baby. It was all so casual and communal.

But that was then and this was now, and this "now" would happen the way Rachel wanted it, and I applauded her for it. At least a part of me did. After all, every woman deserves to give birth in ways that allow her to relax the most. It did not surprise me that my orderly daughter preferred to labor in quiet privacy with her husband, rather than in the middle of a family buffet. But the truth is, I longed to be with her as much as possible during this once-in-a-lifetime event. What mother doesn't? Still, I'd learned from past mistakes to let my adult daughter lead the way, her way.

"I have an idea," I said. "We'll start out driving to Texas, and if we arrive before you go into labor, we'll spend some time with your Granny and Grandpa Arnold until the contractions begin and you head to the hospital. So we'll be close, but not right in your space. How's that sound?"

Rachel added one last caveat, "You promise no one will nag me about when I'm going into labor? As if I would actually *try* to remain pregnant one day longer during the hottest Texas summer on record!"

"Cross my heart, hope to die, stick a boiling thermometer in my eye."

"Okay, then; come on down!"

And so we meandered to Texas, keeping in regular contact by phone. But three days later, Rachel had still not experienced a single serious contraction. So we spent two leisurely days at my mom and dad's comfy ranch home just west of Fort Worth on quaint Lake Granbury (nicknamed "The Ponderosa"), giving Rachel all the wide open space she needed, but close enough to drive to the hospital in an hour at a moment's notice.

Just in case you are wondering if it was hard for me to be so close and yet so far from my daughter who could go into labor at any minute—the answer is a resounding, *Ohmygosh YES!* Every cell in my body wanted to drive straight to her house, show up at her front door, and say, "Surprise! Mama's here!"

But when the desire to go to her uninvited overtook me, Greg confiscated my phone and car keys.

RACHEL

I was miserable. It hurt to sit, it hurt to stand, it hurt to lie down, and thanks to a cold I'd caught earlier in the week and its accompanying bark-like cough, it even hurt to breathe. Oh, and did we mention it was late July in the hottest summer in the history of Texas? We did? Well, it's worth mentioning again. It. Was. *Hot.* I think God knew he had to make the end of pregnancy unbearably uncomfortable to prepare a woman for going through labor. You hit a point when you will do anything, even push a cantaloupe-sized head through your hooha, just to not be pregnant anymore.

By the time my due date rolled around, Jared and I realized our idea of romantically sharing our last days as just-us-two wasn't shaping up like we'd envisioned. "We had four wonderful years of newlywed bliss," I said to Jared, grabbing at my sore throat. "I know we wanted to savor these last days of being alone, but let's be real. These are not days I'll be longing to remember again ... ever. What do you say we call it a wrap?"

"It's been a good run, sweetie," he said, with a compassionate hug. "I know you could use your mom. Go ahead and give her a call."

BECKY

I almost cried with relief when Rachel called to say, "I just crossed out another section to my Early Labor plan. I'm bored to tears. I've also caught some kind of awful cough and cold. I don't feel good, and I need my mama. You and Greg come on over, bring your suitcases, and plan to stay with us, starting now."

There's nothing like feeling needed to kick my inner Mountain Medicine Mama into high gear. "I think Red Raspberry Leaf Tea might get some contractions going," I offered.

"Bring it on," Rachel replied.

Greg and I arrived at Rachel and Jared's house about eight o'clock that evening. I wasted no time after I hugged her miserably swollen self. I stepped into her kitchen, brewed a double strong cup of Red Raspberry Leaf Tea, and sweetened the potion with a dollop of honey. She loved it and asked for another cup. I smiled, knowing my grandbaby would soon be dive-bombing out of Rachel's womb, and we could all commence with the cooing and cuddling that we'd waited nine months to enjoy.

RACHEL

As soon as Mom arrived, she made herself at home in my kitchen, pouring me a cup of kick-start-labor tea in record time.

I eyed her a little suspiciously, not quite trusting this carefree *c'est-la-vie* cook to come onto my carefully organized turf. So I gave her a tour of the kitchen, showing her where I kept cooking essentials and sharing a few kitchen rules.

I held up a green sponge. Exhibit A. "This sponge is *just* for baking sheets; it will scratch glass and nonstick pans. Just stick to the blue one to be on the safe side. Only rinsed dishes go on the right side of the sink, and, for the love of all that is clean, everything *must* be rinsed before going into the dishwasher."

"Wait," Mom said, looking confused, "which sponge is for what? And what qualifies as 'rinsed'?"

"You know, maybe you should write this down," I said. "Rinsed means 'scrubbed with warm water and soap until there's not a trace of food left.'"

Mom scratched her head. "But, Rachey, that sounds like washing, not rinsing. That's why they call it a dish*washer* and not a dish*rinser* ... so you don't have to do all that extra work."

Memories of dishes dotted with dried-on food, from my less-than-antiseptic childhood, sprang to mind. "Mom, the dishwasher is for sanitizing. Come on, I have more to show you before this baby comes. The food processor and rice maker are here. The drawer right below it has the coordinating spatulas for each appliance."

Mom looked in the drawer and grinned. "Oh, yeah, I love those little spatulas, they are handy for lots of little jobs."

"No, no, no, no ... these are kept here for this designated purpose. Rice spoon for rice. Processor spatula for processing. Order in the kitchen, lady!"

There was no doubt about it, if we were two middle-aged men in a 1970s sitcom, my mom would be a stellar Oscar Madison and I would be a shoe-in for Felix Unger of *The Odd Couple*. She is Ernie to my Bert, Lucy to my Ethel, Phoebe to my Monica. I had every intention of coming home from the hospital, giving my mom a day or so to help out (and hopefully not do too much damage), and I'd be back in business, happily cooking up a storm in my own domain, while my newborn slept the days away.

BECKY

The next morning, a day after the official due date, Rachel suspected the tea was working its magic. A previously scheduled appointment with the midwife confirmed our suspicions. The uterus was contracting! Rachel, the Earth Mother, would labor according to her Perfect Plan at home. We respected their privacy, staying nestled on our side of the house, praying for Rachey, for Jared, and for the Baby Who Was Not Yet Named. (I should probably mention here, briefly, that "Name the Baby" was also delayed due to the sudden disappearance of Rachel's decision-making neurons in late pregnancy.)

My baby is having a baby, I thought as the hours ticked by. *It is surprising how happy and natural this feels. All is calm, all is bright* ... Then Jared poked his head into our bedroom about five hours later to deliver a surprising request from Rachel.

RACHEL (EARLIER THAT MORNING)

Nestled into the tub with the lights low, Jacuzzi jets on, and my eyes closed, I listened as a New Age Earth Mama softly whispered affirmations over my iPod: "This is you experiencing you ... Your body knows exactly what to do ... You are a flower in a field opening its petals toward the warmth of the sun ..."

This was going well. My petals were opening. All was calm and serene. The pain was quite manageable ... until it wasn't. Suddenly the contractions were no longer in the category of "strong pressure" as I'd been told to expect. This was a Category-5-hurricane-size contraction.

"I think I want my mom to come with us," I told Jared. "You need to drive, and I may need two hands to squeeze." There are times in a girl's life when she simply needs her mama, and having a baby, I learned, is one of those occasions.

Jared and Greg loaded up the car with his bag, the labor bag, post-labor bag, baby bag, pillows, a Boppy infant feeding pillow, and an ice chest full of juice and vegan snacks. "Just how many weeks are you planning to stay at the hospital?" Greg mused, eyeing the arsenal of supplies. I have to admit, it looked like we were packing for a week-long beach vacation.

Item Number 7 on the "Last Minute Grabs" list had been "Take photo of Jared and me by front door with hospital bag in hand." I'd imagined Jared's arm around me, with smiles of excitement gracing our faces, but there is not enough Max Factor to photo-ready a grimacing woman in intense labor.

I was a woman in the throes of losing control of not only my list, but my ordered life as I once knew it.

Which is, I would soon come to understand, the definition of motherhood.

THE FREEZER IS A MOM'S BEST FRIEND (RECIPES TO FREEZE FOR YOUR FUTURE SELF)
Sweet Potato Pecan Pie Oatmeal Bake

This is one of those dishes I make over and over. It freezes well, transports easily, and is always a crowd pleaser. Since it's already dairy- and egg-free and can easily be made gluten- and soy-free, it's perfect for a crowd with multiple food sensitivities. I also like to bring it to new nursing moms (who are often avoiding at least one of these foods for their baby's sake). —Rachel

Makes 8 large servings (as a main entree) or 16 smaller servings.

Sweet Potato Oatmeal
    4 cups water

4 cups unsweetened almond milk

1 teaspoon salt

4 cups old-fashioned oats (not quick-cooking)

2 cups baked or boiled sweet potato (about 2 large sweet
potatoes) or 15 oz sweet potato puree

1 cup golden raisins (optional)

2 teaspoons cinnamon

4 tablespoons maple syrup (or two ripe bananas to reduce sugar)

Optional: 2 tablespoons chia seeds and an additional cup of
liquid (adds fiber, protein, and healthy omegas; doesn't
change taste or texture as seeds absorb liquid and soften)

Pecan Pie Topping

2 cups chopped pecans

4 tablespoons wheat germ (could replace with flour if you
don't have wheat germ or grind pecans or almonds into
a flour to make it gluten free)

4 tablespoons vegan margarine, such as Earth Balance
(or coconut oil)

4 tablespoons brown sugar

Preheat oven to 400°. In a large sauce pan, bring water, milk, and
salt to a boil. Stir in oatmeal, reduce to medium heat, and add the
remaining ingredients. Cook for about 7 minutes or until most of
the liquid is absorbed. (You could stop now and serve this as is,
and it would be a delicious bowl of oatmeal.) Pour the oatmeal
into one 9x13 or 2 8x8 casserole dishes (or into lined muffin tins
—good for freezing individual servings).

In a small bowl, use your fingers to combine pecans, wheat
germ, brown sugar, and Earth Balance. Sprinkle it over the top
of the oatmeal and bake for 10 minutes or until golden brown and
crunchy on top.

Reheating: Thaw casseroles in refrigerator overnight; cook for
20–30 minutes at 350° in the morning (until heated through).

Broil for the last 2 minutes. Individual muffins can be microwaved for a minute and then crisped under the broiler (remove paper liners) for another minute.

- Vegan/vegetarian
- Gluten free (use gluten-free oats and substitute pecan or almond flour for the wheat germ)

Fresh Corn and Roasted Poblano Chowder

Rachel and I made this one afternoon at her house. She left the room, leaving me careful instructions to watch the homemade croutons that were toasting in the oven for a garnish. The smoke alarms sent her flying back to the kitchen just in time to see her mama running out the back door, carrying a pan covered in square piles of black ash, a trail of smoke following behind. "Just like the good old days," Rachel deadpanned, grabbing a chair and turning off the smoke alarm. Unlike the burnt bread, this soup has just the right kind of smokiness and heat from the roasted poblano peppers and smoked spices, balanced perfectly by the sweet creamy corn. — Becky

Serves 4.

3 cups fresh cooked, grilled, or boiled corn on cob (about 4 large ears)

2 large peppers, cut, seeded, and broiled (skin side up) until blackened and blistered (I used one poblano and one hatch chili — or use peppers of your choice)

1 tablespoon olive oil

1 tablespoon butter or vegan margarine (such as Earth Balance)

1 onion, chopped

2 garlic cloves, minced

1 teaspoon cumin

1 teaspoon smoked paprika

1 teaspoon Hungarian (or regular) paprika

3 cups almond milk

1 cup vegetable broth

1 tablespoon brown sugar

1 teaspoon salt

½ teaspoon pepper

Optional: 1 cup torn kale, sausage (such as Field Roast vegan
  sausages), croutons

Once the cooked corn is cool to touch, cut kernels off the cob into
a bowl, and then rub the knife along the cob again to capture any
"corn milk" juices that you can as well. After rubbing off most of
the charred portion of the skin with a paper towel, dice the roasted
peppers. Melt oil and butter in large, deep skillet or soup pan.
Sauté onions and garlic; add spices, corn, and peppers. Let simmer
over medium-high heat until hot and fragrant, about 3 minutes.
Add almond milk, vegetable broth, salt, pepper, and sugar. Simmer until hot and bubbly, stirring regularly.

Carefully ladle half of the soup mixture into a food processor
or blender and blend until smooth. Pour back into pan and stir
into the waiting corn-pepper-spice mixture, until just reheated.
Check to see if it needs more salt and adjust seasonings to your
liking. If freezing, let cool and pour into labeled Ziploc bags or
freezer-safe containers at this point. Defrost and heat until warm
and add any of the optional additions below.

Optional: Add about a cup of torn kale to soup after you stir
the blended portion into the other half (or when reheating), and
cook until kale is tender. Toast up some bread cubes under the
broiler for quick croutons. Slice and brown sausages in a little olive
oil. Sprinkle atop the soup to make it a hearty one-bowl meal.

Omnivore Options: Use dairy milk to replace almond milk and
chicken broth to replace vegetable broth if you prefer. Drizzle with
heavy cream, sour cream, or Greek yogurt, or sprinkle with cheese
and crisp bacon.

- *Vegan/vegetarian*
- *Gluten free*

Coconut-Covered Cherry Freezer Bites

If life is just a bowl of cherries, I want my life to be a bowl of these coconut-covered cherry bites. It would be a sweet and bright life, full of health and energy and little bites of bliss that make you stop and say, "Wow," "Mmmm," and "More please." I like to keep a bowl of these in my freezer at all times, because every day needs at least one wow moment. —Rachel

Note: *When full fat coconut milk gets cold, the coconut water settles at the bottom of the can, leaving a thick cream at the top. If you open the can upside down, you can just pour the liquid out (save or freeze it for smoothies) and scoop out the cream.*

Makes about 15 Cherries.

2 tablespoons cream from full fat coconut milk that has been refrigerated for at least an hour (avoid coconut milk with preservatives or it may not separate)

1 teaspoon sugar

¼ teaspoon vanilla extract

15 frozen or fresh pitted cherries

parchment or wax paper

In a bowl, mix coconut cream, sugar, and vanilla until the sugar dissolves. Dip the frozen cherries into the cream a few at a time and place on a parchment- or wax-paper lined pan. If the cream isn't sticking well, pat the cherries dry with a paper towel. Place in the freezer for 20–30 minutes until the cream coating is completely frozen. Transfer to air tight zip-top bag or container. Enjoy straight from the freezer.

Variations:

Add 1 teaspoon cocoa powder for chocolate covered cherries.
Use banana slices with a maple-cinnamon coconut dip.
Roll in sprinkles or shredded coconut.

• Vegan/vegetarian
• Gluten free

Chapter 6

Unto Us a Baby Texan Is Born

The moment a child is born,
the mother is also born.

Rajneesh

BECKY

We drove away, with Jared at the wheel, me in the backseat, and Rachel, heavy with child and pain, in the front seat. I suppressed the desire to dance the Mommy Jig at this point, so happy was I to get to play a real supporting role in my daughter's labor! But when I saw the grimace and pain on Rachel's face, the only thing I thought was, "Lord, get my girl out of pain!"

As we exited the driveway she warned me — and this is an exact quote, though I don't know if she will remember it — "Mom, I might cuss. I've been watching a lot of *The Kardashians* lately." Indeed, as the drive to the hospital unfolded, we discovered she'd learned lots of interesting phrases from those Kardashian girls.

En route, the contractions increased to barely a minute apart, and all attempts at levity disappeared in the wake of my efforts to help her breathe and get through the pain. Soon she was in a state of agony that tugged at every mother nerve in my body. Jared, bless him, was the most amazing husband and labor coach a woman could ask for. My love for him (already pretty darn strong) deepened even more every time he looked in her frightened eyes, took her hand, and calmly said, "Just breathe, baby. You're doing great." And she did, and she was. To know your child is married to a man who loves her this much, who will cherish and protect her with every fiber of his body, the way I had once done for her as a little girl, is a gift I do not take lightly.

I followed Jared's lead and stayed quiet and calm until, as we neared the hospital, Rachel announced that she felt the urge to push. With the intensity and frequency of the contractions, I truly thought I might end up delivering her baby in the front seat of the car. And if so, I was prepared.

Years before, when Rachel was born during a Texas ice storm, by the time I'd convinced my then-husband that I was truly in labor, her head had crowned. Her father delivered her, and I suctioned her mouth myself, helping her to take her first breath. The midwife arrived about forty-five minutes later. I felt confident that if it came down to it, I could totally deliver my daughter's baby. Mercifully, my emergency skills would not be needed. Jared pulled into the Pregnant Woman Drop-Off Zone, the wheels coming to a halting screech. I jumped out, dashed into the hospital, ran down the corridor straight to the labor-and-delivery area and, like a maniac, shouted to everyone within earshot, "My daughter's about to have a baby in the parking lot! She wants to push! Help! Help!"

Within seconds, two nurses appeared with a wheelchair and followed me out to the parking lot where they put Rachel in the chair and then wheeled her expertly into a labor room. The time was about 5:00 p.m. I collapsed into the nearest chair in the waiting room and began doing my own Lamaze breathing to calm myself down for my daughter's sake.

RACHEL

After the arduous journey to the hospital, I was sure I'd be meeting my baby boy any minute. Cecily, my midwife, walked into the labor room with a comforting smile. She was that perfect combination of boho Earth Mother and confident medical professional. She inspired both calm and confidence with her medical jacket over her gypsy skirt. After doing a quick exam, Cecily announced cheerily, "You are five centimeters dilated."

Five? Just five? But that's only half-way there, I thought, fighting back a wave of discouragement.

I knew I needed to stay positive, so as soon as I was taken off the monitors, I asked to get in the hospital's tub. I felt sure if I could just get in a warm tub of water, I could get back to opening my petals in a relaxing, less-agonizing calm.

Cecily poured water over my lower back where the pain was the worst and encouraged me to relax between contractions, but honestly, there didn't seem to be any "between." After a few contractions that literally twisted my entire body out of the bathtub, I announced that I was ready to negotiate. An epidural was sounding mighty tempting. Despite assurances from Cecily that this was a good decision and might actually help my body relax enough to move the birth along faster, I felt defeated and betrayed by my body, embarrassed that I couldn't handle what women had been doing for centuries without the aid of pain relief.

A short, cheerful man in a white doctor's coat appeared with the goods, and while k.d. lang crooned a slow and somber "Hallelujah" over my iPod speakers, he administered the epidural. Soon, the pain vanished completely. Hallelujah indeed.

After a little rest, I was stricken with an unquenchable thirst. The nurses later told me I cleaned out the entire Labor and Delivery Ward's stock of apple juice (the ones in the little plastic cup with a tin lid that you pull back). They were chilled to a perfect slushy consistency, just to the point where the small ice chunks dissolve as soon as you take a sip and so cold that you feel the frostiness of it go across your tongue and all the way down your throat.

Since food memories are some of the most lasting, the taste

of cold apple juice will forever bring me back to that long night waiting for my baby to arrive, and remind me of the refreshing energy I felt when, between contractions, Jared offered me that little plastic cup, thoughtfully holding the straw to my lips.

BECKY

Soon after sitting down in the waiting room, I called Rhonda, Jared's mom, and told her we might have a grandbaby soon, judging by the intensity of Rachel's contractions. This would be the first grandchild born on Jared's side of the family. I should also mention that there is no occasion in Jared's large, chatty, fun-loving Texas-drawlin' family that goes uncelebrated. I'm pretty sure Groundhog Day is cause for Jim, Jared's dad, to haul a beef quarter out of the freezer to be rubbed, seasoned, smoked, and grilled for twenty-four hours and served alongside a bathtub full of Ranch Style beans and hot tub full of Rotel Cheese Dip for the dozens of relatives arriving from hither and yon. Nana, the adorable matriarch of the Randolph clan, and often the hostess of the family parties, can typically be spotted near the crackers (she "loves a good cracker!") and boxed Zin that she enjoys with a floating ice cube, grinning and having more fun than an elf at Christmas. Needless to say, the birth of the first grandchild had caused no shortage of Randolph excitement.

It seemed that Rhonda had barely finished saying, "I'm drivin' over right now!" before she walked into the hospital waiting room, flanked by her youngest boy, a good-natured fifteen-year-old named Jayce. He'd been playing baseball and was still in his uniform, looking a little bewildered to have been jerked off the field only to find himself plopped in a maternity waiting room.

Soon the rest of the Randolph clan arrived to take up half the waiting room, so we set up camp, with snacks and card games and frequent cell-phone checks, anticipating the announcement of our unnamed grandson's arrival at any moment.

When Jared told us that Rachel had received an epidural, it was as though someone had injected my brain with euphoric pain relievers as well. Her labor pains had been much more intense than mine had been at this point, and I had prayed fervently that she'd choose relief. Rhonda and I got to go back and hug Rachel, who was feeling amazingly chipper after the good, good medicine made the bad, bad pain go away.

By midnight, there was still no baby, but we did get word that Rachel had just started pushing.

One hour passed with no news. I was nervous but okay.

Two hours passed, still no word. My concern rose, but I remembered it took me three hours to push my first child out into the world.

RACHEL

Around midnight, Cecily confirmed it was "go time," but because of meconium in the waters, as soon as my child was born he'd need deep suctioning by a medical team. My heart sank a little further as another set of treasured plans were foiled. I wouldn't get to hold and nurse my baby immediately. His first breath would not come while in my arms; his first moments in this world would not be next to me, hearing the familiar beat of my heart.

I struggled against these fresh waves of disappointment and focused on the goal ahead: get this baby born.

A team of nurses arrived who would help tend to the baby, and they stood about four feet from the end of my bed, like an audience waiting for the show to begin. *Fantastic.* They sang and danced along to my birth soundtrack, even shouted out a few song requests. I was tempted to offer them refreshments of slushy apple juice and an oatmeal raisin muffin from my cooler stash, but it's hard to be a suave hostess when you're hooked up to IVs and monitors.

After the clock had ticked off an hour's worth of minutes, I could see "the audience" yawning and twiddling their thumbs. It's always disheartening when your guests seem bored at a party, and I felt even more pressure to get the star of the show out on stage —ASAP.

At this point, it appeared I just needed a few good pushes to deliver the little rock star to his awaiting fans. I pushed for another *hour* and still nada. I was officially the most boring entertainer on the L&D floor.

As we "laboriously" entered the third hour, my lingering chest cold started acting up, and I began having an impressive coughing fit. Cecily excitedly said, "Do that again!" and I let out another big cough, which was followed by a frenzy of excitement. Within a blur of seconds, a tiny little human was laying on my belly. I literally coughed my baby into the world.

Jared cut the cord, and I cried as I stroked my son's black hair and softly touched his puffy rosy cheeks. "There you are," I whispered to him. So this was the little boy I'd been feeling in my belly for months, the little bean that had stolen my appetite for vegetables and greens and replaced it with cravings for Oriental Ramen Noodles and tortilla wrapped pickles dipped in buffalo sauce. The little guy I'd planned for, prayed over, dreamed of. What would I name this bundle of preciousness?

But before I could think another thought, my baby boy was whisked out of my arms by the waiting medical team to make sure his lungs were clear. Jared leaned over, kissed my forehead, and whispered, "You did great, baby. I'm so proud of you."

"Thank you," I said as I looked up at my husband, and now also the father of my child. "Will you go be with our son? I'll be fine."

And as I said, "I'll be fine," I knew it would be true. My baby was healthy and the most beautiful thing I'd ever seen in my life.

My husband loved me and was proud of me.

To heck with Birth Plans. I had a brand new son to love. He had no name, but he was here and he was ours. And that's all that mattered in that moment when the world shifted within, and I turned from being a Woman with an Agenda to a Mother with Child.

BECKY

After three hours passed and still no word, I was officially panicky and close to tears. Not wanting to worry Jared's family, I asked Greg to walk with me to the car. Once there, I collapsed, crying into his arms as he prayed for Rachel, the baby, Jared, and my anxious heart. Just as he said amen my cell phone buzzed. There was a text from Rhonda: "We may have a baby."

I flew back to the waiting room on the wings of Relieved Mama euphoria. Rhonda had never let worry or concern cross her face during the long wait, and I'd tried hard to follow her lead. But when we received a text with a picture of our newborn grandson's face, we grabbed each other and sobbed with relief, gratitude, and joy, blubbering, "I was *so* worried!" and the other echoing, "I was too!"

Once I kissed the exhausted, proud, glowing, incredibly gorgeous face of my daughter-turned-mother, I was free to gaze into the sweetest black eyes in Texas. Is there anything like the knowing, innocent wide-eyed gaze of a baby freshly arrived from the hand of God? He was perfect, from his dark hair (which looked like he'd stopped off at the barber on his way out of the womb) to his beautiful long toes. He was also a surprisingly heavy arm full. Since Rachel had only gained sixteen pounds and looked like a cover model for *Beautiful Pregnancy* magazine, we were expecting she'd deliver a little tyke. This hefty fellow weighed in at eight pounds, four ounces!

Joyful but exhausted, we turned from Rachel and the baby to thank and hug the best son-in-law in the world, now the best-new-father-in-the-world. Greg and I left the hospital arm in arm, two limp noodles of relief, and slept until noon the next day.

RACHEL

It was five o'clock in the morning before we said goodbye to our last visitors. With a swaddled baby sleeping deeply in the crook of my arm, I carefully unwrapped a homemade No-Bake Apricot Bar from my snack stash (the recipe is at the end of Chapter 11). I hadn't eaten in almost a day and my brain was screaming for food, food, food! The tart apricot layered between salty rich cashews made the perfect bite: crunchy and gooey, savory and sweet. It was just the refueling I needed after a hard night's work.

Now that I'd had some nourishment, I began to think more clearly. Jared and I sat and gazed at our little man, then began discussing what we should call him.

I didn't just get stalled choosing a name because I was scatter-brained. I got stalled because naming a child seemed monumental and permanent. It's the name he will have to share every time he meets someone new, the name he puts on his résumé, the name that will be announced as he walks up to bat or across the graduation stage.

The previous summer, as we were strolling the Strand in Galveston, we'd heard a mother call out to an adorable little boy. We had turned to each other at the same time and said, "I love that name!" We wrote it down on our short list of future baby name possibilities.

Not only did I agonize over the first name, but there was also the issue of the middle name. Jared wanted it to be *Ray*, a family name belonging to both Jared and his dad. However meaning-ful to the Randolphs, *Ray* had seemed too simple, too lacking in creativity. And since most of the top names on our list all began with *J*, my Texas born son's initials would be *JR*—just a little too *Dallas* for my taste.

However, during the time when I was being stitched up and the nurses were suctioning our baby, I observed something that changed my mind in an instant. Our son was screaming from all the procedures (which tore at my heart), but when the nurse handed the baby to Jared, he bounced his son's tightly swaddled body, softly whispering "shhh" into his ear, and our boy grew instantly quiet, staring up at his daddy, wide-eyed and calm. He seemed to know he was in good hands.

In that very moment, passing down the middle name Ray no longer felt like an obligation; it became an honor. Jared was a daddy, and a darn good one at that. I was suddenly proud to pass along the Randolph legacy. The middle name decided, we quickly agreed to go with the first name that floated to the top of our list that day in Galveston. It was an old classic that had stood the test of time—and it had a nice ring to it when I practiced using my best Southern accent to holler him home. We pretended calling him to bat, handing him his diploma, introducing him to a future employer. We agreed, our son would have a hard time failing in life, with such a good, strong name.

A good name is better than fine perfume.

Ecclesiastes 7:1

BECKY

Once fully awake and caffeinated the next morning, Greg and I drove to the hospital, hugged the new mom and dad, and then took our turns having our pictures made with the Hit of the Parade, along with the three thousand other relatives who were waiting in line behind us. When I held the Unnamed Child, breathing in his sweet newborn scent, I noticed he had a deep dimple on his sweet, soft-as-a-ripe-peach right cheek. I will be bragging on the fact that "I was the first one to notice he has a dimple!" until he is in his fifties, when I will insert it casually into every conversation. "Yes, my grandson is running for president of the United States. But did you realize ... I am the one who first noticed he has a dimple?"

Soon Jim and Rhonda and their sons (now proud new uncles), along with Nana and Papa, Jared's grandparents, arrived. Nana, the Zin-and-cracker-lovin' grandmother, is married to an equally adorable husband, Papa. Picture the cutest grandma and grandpa you can possibly conjure up in your mind from any of your favorite fairy tales, and let me tell you, they will look like a pair of gangstas next to Nana and Papa. Nana's eyes are always sparkling like a child who is about to open a present. (She once charmed *the* Ernest Hemingway when she was a youthful newlywed living in the Florida Keys, where Papa was stationed in the Navy. Ernest called her his "Texas Tornado.") You can imagine, if she can almost hyperventilate with joy over a well-baked Ritz, the thrill she was feeling over her new great-grandson.

Jared interrupted the roar of oohs and aahs coming forth from the madding crowd in the hospital room to make an announcement in his good-natured Texas twang. "Okay, y'all! Rach and I have some news you've all been waiting to hear."

At this Nana chirped, "Wait! Everybody get in a circle and let's all hold hands before you tell us anything, Jared."

"Nana, we're not going to pray or anything," Jared said. "I'm just going to tell you what we've decided to name the baby."

Nana took my hand and nodded for the rest of us to form the family circle, which we all did on cue. "I know, honey, but it's more dramatic this way." She grinned, her eyes twinkling, as she added, "And we *love* drama!"

Jared cleared his throat. "Rachel and I have decided to name our son ... Jackson Ray Randolph."

This was followed by claps, hugs, kisses, and enthusiastic comments of approval. Rachel mimicked a trailer-trash mama to demonstrate how practical his name was for hollering purposes: "Jackson Ray Randolph, you get yur butt in the house right now!"

"Wow," I said, "that's good. And it's kind of spooky how well you do that."

My father loved the name, telling me in an email later that it sounded like a dignified Southern general. And now that we could see our grandson's face, it was perfectly clear. Jackson was simply the right name for this precious boy with knowing black eyes, an adorable dimple, and a future of being spoiled beyond his wildest dreams by grandmothers and great-grandmothers who will never see him as anything but perfect, flawless, and amazing his whole life long.

I could hardly wait to share a toast with Rhonda and Nana later as we bragged on the most beautiful baby in the world, enjoying a good cracker, and washing it down with a glass of lukewarm boxed Zin with an ice cube floating on top.

CELEBRATION RECIPES

"Carrot Cake" Chutney and Cream Cheese Topping for Nana's Beloved Crackers

Years ago, for my birthday, my sister sent me a jar of Carrot Cake Chutney from a gourmet specialty store with instructions to plop a bit on top of a good cracker with cream cheese. It was heavenly and left a taste memory for years. Recently I tried my hand at recreating it, and by golly, I think I did it! —Becky

Makes about 1¼ cups.

> 5 medium-sized organic carrots peeled, rough chopped to ready for food processor
>
> ⅓ cup well-drained crushed pineapple
>
> ⅓ cup agave nectar
>
> 1 tablespoon brown sugar
>
> pinch of salt
>
> ½ teaspoon vanilla
>
> 2 teaspoons cinnamon
>
> 3 tablespoons raisins
>
> 2 tablespoons white vinegar

Process carrots in a food processor or blender to a tiny dice (as you would for a carrot salad). Mix the carrots with all the remaining ingredients and simmer in a skillet on medium low for about 5 to 8 minutes or until the carrots are tender crisp and the syrup is thick and reduced by at least half, most of it absorbed into the carrots and raisins, with only a tablespoon or two of syrup remaining in pan. If you'd like your chutney to have a bit more kick to it, add another teaspoon of vinegar or a squeeze of fresh lemon once you've removed the pan from the burner. Cool and put in a tightly covered container in the fridge to let the flavors mingle and intensify. Serve cold with a small spoon, alongside a plate of crackers and a small bowl of whipped cream cheese.

• Vegetarian

- Vegan (serve with vegan cream cheese)
- Gluten free (serve with rice crackers)

Bourbon Brown Sugar Pork Loin

This is Greg's favorite main dish, and guests swoon over it so much that I never use any other recipe for pork loin. Pork never had it so happy, swimming in bourbon, butter, and brown sugar—who wouldn't be tender? The bonus is that it is also fabulously easy and fast to cook. —Becky

Serves 3 to 4 (easily doubled for a bigger group).

1 small pork tenderloin

1½ teaspoons Cajun seasoning (I like Tony Chachere's brand)

1 tablespoon olive oil

1 tablespoon butter

1 tablespoon brown sugar

¼ cup bourbon, whiskey, or scotch

Heat oven to 350°. Rub the pork tenderloin all over with Cajun seasoning. Put oil and butter into an iron skillet (or other oven-proof skillet) over high heat. Once the oil is very hot, put the tenderloin into the pan, turning heat down a bit, and brown until golden on all sides, turning with tongs. Don't worry about getting it done in the middle; just get it pretty and brown on the outside. Remove pan from heat. Sprinkle brown sugar and pour bourbon all over and roll the tenderloin in the juices now in the pan. Cover lightly with foil and place in oven. Cook for about 25 minutes or until just done in the middle. Pork loin is often overcooked and this is what makes it tough. If you have a meat thermometer, cook until it registers 140°. Remove from oven. Let it sit for at least 5 minutes, covered to let juices redistribute.

Slice just before serving in thin slices, ladling a little of the pan juices over it. Delicious with baked sweet potatoes and a green veggie or salad.

Vegan Variation: This method can also be used to cook slices of tofu. Just do not cover it when you put it in the oven and remove earlier, after about 10 minutes.

- Vegan (see variation above)
- Gluten free (those with extreme celiac disease may react to bourbon, but most are fine with it)

Mama's All Natural (No Sugar) Apple Crisp Skillet

Every cook needs at least one "no sugar" recipe to keep on hand for people who have sworn off the white stuff. This apple crisp is the perfect answer; no one will suspect there is no sugar within. —*Becky*

Apple Layer

2 tablespoons butter or vegan margarine, such as Earth Balance

2 tablespoons coconut sugar

2 tablespoons maple syrup

1 teaspoon cinnamon

3 cups fresh organic apple slices, loosely packed, ¼ inch thick, peel left on (about 5 small apples or 3 large apples)

2 tablespoons raisins or dried berries

Topping

1 cup old-fashioned oats

½ cup walnuts

2 tablespoons hemp, chia, or flax seeds

¼ cup coconut oil (or grape-seed oil, butter, or margarine)

3 tablespoons coconut sugar

¼ teaspoon salt (unless nuts above are salted, then omit)

1 teaspoon cinnamon

1 tablespoon pure maple syrup

Optional: 2 tablespoons roasted pumpkin seeds for garnish (or sunflower seeds or slivered almonds)

Preheat oven to 350°. In a 10-inch iron skillet, melt butter over a low flame. Mix rest of apple-layer ingredients into the melted butter. Put all topping ingredients, except the maple syrup, into a food processor. Process until mixture is crumbly, about the size of Grape Nuts cereal. Sprinkle over the apples. Drizzle 1 tablespoon of maple syrup over all. Bake at 350° for about 30 minutes or until topping is brown, apples are soft, and juices beneath are thick and syrupy. Top with pumpkin seeds, if desired. Serve plain or with a scoop of vanilla ice cream, yogurt, or coconut milk–based ice cream.

- *Vegetarian*
- *Vegan (use Earth Balance)*
- *Gluten free (use gluten-free oats)*

No Stress Sangrias

My son, Gabe, an excellent cook, served this to me one hot July afternoon on his back porch, alongside a delicious grilled lunch. I could not believe it was so easy, and it fast became my favorite summer cocktail. —Becky

1 part chilled lemon-lime or grapefruit soda

1 part chilled Merlot or Cabernet

slices of citrus

Ice

In a glass or pitcher, mix equal parts soda and red wine. Mix with ice and any slices of citrus you like. That's it!

- *Vegan/vegetarian*
- *Gluten free*

Chapter 7

Walmart Gourmet

To truly comfort,
a food must function like a hug from your mother.
It makes you feel all better.
Bonny Wolf

BECKY

"What are you doing?" Greg called from Rachel and Jared's kitchen. "The kids just called, and they are on their way home from the hospital with the new baby!"

"I'm in Rachel's office, looking for stuff to make a 'Welcome Home Jackson' sign!" Drawing on my degree in Elementary Education (with master's work in Early Childhood Specialization), I taped several colorful index cards together with ribbon and tinsel and decorated them with colored markers and stickers. In five minutes the handmade sign was on the front door. I stepped back to admire my handiwork. Perfect. It looked exactly as though a Kindergartener had made it. I'm so thankful my college education was not a waste.

The new parents pulled up in the driveway, and Greg and I rushed to help them out of the car. Jared helped Rachel, gingerly, from the front seat. She looked beautiful, but it wouldn't take a mother's intuition to see that she was also weak, sore, and in need of a soft place to land her tired, achy body. Next came baby Jackson, sleeping like an angel in his car seat. His bangs, still looking freshly trimmed, framed his silky soft face, and made him appear especially dapper for his debut. Now and again, he'd sigh in his sleep, and I'd catch a glimpse of his deep dimple and of course, cuddle him close, and give him a kiss to bless it.

Next followed the never-ending unloading parade: ice chests, bags, suitcases, special pillows, and diaper bag—enough stuff to have provided Rach and Jared sustenance and comfort for not only a hospital stay, but probably a nuclear fallout.

The first night was a little rough, as first nights with newborns and exhausted new moms tend to be. At one point, hearing crying down the hall, I met Rachel at her bedroom door. I took one look at her and for a moment wondered whether the cries had come from the baby or his mother. She had that brand-new-mom look, resembling a recent escapee from an asylum: disheveled, exhausted, and at the end of her strength. I held out my arms to receive the bundle of squirmy wide-awake baby boy. He was already straining to hold his wobbly newborn head up to take in everything around him, like a bobble-head in a blanket.

"I think he's full, but he just won't settle down and sleep," Rachel said wearily, holding back tears from sheer exhaustion after all she'd been through in the last forty-eight hours.

"You go back to bed and rest," I assured her. "Jackson and I need some bonding time. Besides, I have some writing due tomorrow. He'll keep me company."

I padded down the hall to the living room with my new grandson in my arms, his black eyes open and gazing with wonder as if to say, "Where the heck am I? Can anybody around here tell me what's going on?" I did my best to communicate the answers I felt he was seeking in my best baby-talk-eze. "You are da fweetest wittle baby in Texas, and I am your Nonny who will love you foreber!" (Kiss on his forehead.) "You are in a safe, good, happy pwace with your sweet mom and dad." (Peck on each cheek.) "You will like it here. I pwomise."

Jackson stared back in fascination, as if he was starting to understand, and began to relax. I cuddled him in my right arm and settled into a big easy chair with my laptop positioned so I could both hold him and write a blog that was due the next morning. (I had taken a freelance job writing about how to keep aging brains young, a subject suddenly near and dear to my heart.) Jackson loved the light of the computer; an hour later he was dozing sweetly, and I was finished with my work. His mom got a little bit of sleep before he woke, ready for his next wee-hours-of-the-morning snack. The next morning, we did the handoff again, and after some time of communing together, baby Jackson once again settled into the crook of my arms to watch me write until he dozed off. I dubbed him my Little Writing Buddy, sure that one day he'd thank me for this jumpstart in journalism when he wins a Pulitzer.

Besides still recovering from a bad cold and cough, Rachel had lost a lot of blood during her long labor, just as I had done with my first birth. The plan was that I would stay for about four days to help, and then she was sure she'd be up and ready to take over the reins of her own home, kitchen, and baby again. In reality, she was doing all she could to take control of nursing the baby, brushing her teeth and hair, and finding a semi-comfortable way to sit upright.

Greg had to get back to Denver, so he drove home, planning to fly me back in a few days, via a one-way ticket.

Rocking the baby now and then was pure delight, so the only real challenge for me was to figure out how to cook for vegans, using what I could scrounge up at the produce aisle at the local small town Walmart. Rachel's freezer was full of those home-cooked meals she'd made during her nesting streak, but I wanted her to save those for when she and Jared were alone and when I would not be around to help in the kitchen. Needless to say, a Texas-based Walmart has limited choices for plant-based eaters, but I like a cooking challenge. I just pretended I was on a redneck version of the show *Chopped*, where chefs have to create gourmet meals out of a basket of weird ingredients like turnip greens, jicama, an Asian piglet, cough syrup, and Fruit Loops.

I looked forward to my little Walmart excursion every day. I'd ask Rach what she was in the mood for; then I'd create a recipe in my head, make a list, and drive off in search of the ingredients. (One item, of course, was always on the menu: Jared's beloved guacamole and salsa.)

Jackson was a strong and hearty nursing baby, gulping down the calories from Rachel's body as fast as she could produce them. Thus, she was ravenous all the time. What stuns me about Rachel, and vegans in general, is the amount of food they can put away. It may all be veggies and grains and beans and seeds, but they can eat mounding plates full, like field hands, and never get fat. This intrigued me. I decided that "while in Rome" I would eat vegan meals right along with the natives and see what happened.

A parade of guests from our large extended families came and went steadily, in small herds, those first few days to ooh and ahh at the new little prince. One of them brought a large, gorgeous Bundt cake. Lemon and blueberry, loaded with rich, thick, icing. Because Rachel and Jared could not eat it (it had eggs and butter in it), I began supplementing my experimental vegan diet with large slabs of cake. So much for any hope of getting thin in a week.

The day before I was to leave for Denver, I found Rachel huddled up with her new baby, gazing at him in profound mother-love. She looked up at me, tears rimming her eyes. "Mom, I don't want to hurt anybody's feelings, but I really, really want a relaxed day alone with you and the baby tomorrow."

I smiled at her, waves of relief and love pulsing in my heart. It took all my self-control not to do a little tap-dance of joy. *My daughter loves me. She needs me. She wants some mom–daughter–new-baby bonding time. Alone.*

"Whatever you need and want, you got it," I said. Then I turned to make phone calls to free up our last day alone, together.

RACHEL

Despite utter exhaustion and major discomfort lingering from giving birth, my new role as momma-to-Jackson could not have felt more natural. He conformed to my body perfectly. I had held other newborns and struggled to find the right way to hold them, but it was different with my own son. We fit like two connecting puzzle pieces. His head lay perfectly in the crevice of my elbow, his legs draped around my belly, still soft and "comfortable" from pregnancy, and his hands folded neatly on his chest in what Mom and I dubbed "his prayer hands." As he got tired, he turned toward my body and tucked his head into the dark cave of my armpit, unfolding his prayer hands and tucking one little fist by his face and laying the other on my chest.

I could gaze at him for days, and in fact, because my mom was there to take care of housework and meals, I pretty much got to do just that. While the steady flow of visitors coming to see and hold Jackson was flattering, I discovered what I needed as a new mother, more than anything, was someone to prepare a meal that I could eat one-handed while rocking and nursing my baby.

On one of Mom's first Walmart trips, she purchased a set of wooden TV dinner trays. She set up one in front of my rocking chair, and from then on she served my breakfast, lunch, and dinner there while Jackson nuzzled in the crook of one arm. There's something about food on TV trays that symbolizes pure pampering to me. Granny, my mom's mother, loved to spoil me when I was a little girl by serving our lunches on TV trays. They were made of aluminum with collapsible legs, sporting pictures of baby animals. In a family that didn't watch a lot of television, eating on TV trays was an extra special treat, reserved for those "spoiling" days when we were allowed to watch endless *I Love Lucy* reruns (or these days, back-to-back episodes of *How I Met Your Mother*) while curled up on the couch (or now, with my baby in the rocker).

I asked Mom if Granny indulged her this same way. Mom smiled in remembrance. "Your Granny was a champion post-baby pamperer. She would serve me healthy, beautiful meals in bed, beginning just hours after I gave birth, so all I had to think about was resting and nursing a newborn. Granny told me that some of *her* best memories are of Nonny, your great-grandmother, doing the very same thing for her, traveling on a Greyhound bus from Sweetwater to Dallas, with her apron packed in her suitcase."

I come from a long line of nurturing women, and I'm sure when it is my turn to care for a convalescing loved one, it will be second nature for me to know what to do.

Mom and I laughed as she took away my lunch tray, noting that Jackson's sleepers were covered in an equal mix of muffin crumbs, guacamole, and spit up.

With Greg gone and Jared back at work full-time, it wasn't long before us women found our rhythm. Mom snuggled with Jackson in the morning while I attempted to catch up on sleep. By the time Jackson was hungry and ready for his breakfast, I was ready for mine too. We settled into our rocking chair feeding zone. Jackson gulped his breakfast while Mom popped a couple of whole-wheat waffles (homemade from my freezer frenzy stash) under the broiler. Since Mom still isn't a morning person, the frozen breakfast foods, like waffles, Powerhouse Muffins, and Sweet Potato Oatmeal Bake, came in handy. She slathered the waffles with peanut butter, sliced bananas, and warm maple syrup, the way I like it. Handing me my breakfast, she asked, "Now then. What would you like for lunch?" "The Next Meal" is a topic we never tire of discussing, and it is never too soon to bring it up.

"How about rice bowls? Remember the ones you served for the Girls' Night when I was at your house last summer?" I asked.

"Oh, those are so easy. Really, I'll make you anything you want."

"But that *is* what I want. Will you sauté some veggies to go on top?"

"Absolutely. At least you're not asking me to drive you through McDonald's."

We both grinned at the memory. On my twelfth birthday, Mom drove the two of us all the way to the big city of Dallas to celebrate my special day together. She took us to an enormous metropolitan bookstore, expecting we'd both browse for an hour or so. In fifteen minutes, I'd picked out a couple of thin books and a teen magazine and was itching to go. Then Mom gave me a choice between going to a lady's tea room or a la-di-da restaurant for lunch. I told her what I really wanted was to go to McDonald's. And since it was my birthday, and my choice, we did.

"I have to take some of the blame," Mom admitted. "With all the Happy Meals I fed you back in those days when I was juggling four kids and a career, I am not sure you knew what real food outside a bun, bag, or box even tasted like."

"I know," I chimed in. "My idea of fine dining was ordering a drive-through meal that wasn't on the Dollar Menu. I had a pretty limited culinary horizon. But, hey, I love cooking now and so do all my brothers, so maybe there's something to the 'fend for yourself' training method."

"Well, I'm going to start making up for all those fast-food meals. Say hello to your personal chef for the week. Now, will you two be okay while I make a quick run to the store for rice bowl ingredients?"

"We'll be fine," I reassured her. "I think I'll try to make a dent in unpacking my hospital bags today."

Mom's daily trips to Walmart were like little trial runs, previews of what it would be like when she wouldn't be around to help. It was hard not to feel shockingly discouraged at this point. Most days, my big accomplishment, beyond nursing and changing Jackson, was to take a shower. If my stamina held, I might also start a load of laundry. Though Mom reminded me that my birth was long and the loss of blood meant loss of extra energy, I was unprepared for the extreme exhaustion and weakness, alongside the lack of sleep. I prayed for a quick recovery and asked God to give me the strength I'd need to take care of my baby alone; but in truth, I was worried. I was also flooded with compassion for women who don't have moms or close friends to care for them in the early days following birth, especially if their husbands have to return to work soon. How do they manage?

During the time Mom was gone, I managed to unload just one bag while Jackson chilled in his bouncy chair nearby. As soon as she returned with her haul, she set to work in the kitchen. The rice bubbled in the rice maker. I could hear her knife hitting the board — chop chop chop chop — as she sliced zucchini and squash into thin strips. Oil sizzled when the veggies slid into the hot pan. I could close my eyes and, from my rocking chair perch, imagine everything Mom was doing in the kitchen. I also closed my eyes because I dared not look at the dozens of my kitchen rules she was sure to be breaking. Still, my ears caught the sounds of mischief-making. I heard a soft scraping sound and knew Mom was using the non-heat proof plastic rice maker spoon to scoop the veggies from the skillet. I heard her load the dishwasher, but I didn't hear any water running, signaling the awful truth: *Unrinsed dishes were going into my dishwasher.*

But I was hungry and still too weak to protest, to tell my mother once more that there's a specific utensil for each cooking task, and that my dishwasher is not a power car wash. Or that "cleaning as you go" really saves time in the long run. Of perhaps more concern was that I really didn't even care all that much. The Tired Mom part of me had overtaken my inner OCD Mom, lazily responding to all of it, *Oh, well. Whatever.*

Any remaining vestiges of anxiety relaxed into a smile when Mom walked in with my meal, announcing with a flourish,

"Madame, your lunch is served!" I hungrily eyed the bowl of snowy jasmine rice topped with sautéed vegetables seasoned in Bragg's Aminos (a soy-like sauce packed with more nutrition) and a touch of sesame oil. A sprinkle of toasted sliced almonds and green onions decorated the top.

My taste buds were happy. I'd think about the disorder in my kitchen tomorrow.

Chasing the last piece of rice around the bowl with my fork, I hollered into the kitchen, "More please!"

"My goodness, Little Mama, you've got quite the appetite. Coming up!"

Mom was true to her promise to make up for all those drive-through meals of my childhood. She was totally in her Paula-Deen-Gone-Vegan Zone and announced she was going for an Around the World Vegan theme for the week. One night was Mexican food: homemade refried beans on tortillas with roasted veggies and guacamole with a side of Spanish rice. On Italian night she pan-fried thin slices of eggplant (that had been coated in crispy panko breadcrumbs) and served them atop a mound of spaghetti with marinara for a crispier version of Eggplant Parmesan. Even Jared, a once confirmed eggplant-hater, scarfed it down. Greek night was warmed fresh pitas, homemade hummus, and a Greek salad of cucumbers, tomatoes, pepperoncinis, olives, and vinaigrette with lemon and oregano. On American Theme Night, Mom was frustrated when her attempt at homemade veggie burgers looked more like poop-in-a-pan. Veggie burgers, to her credit, are tricky to make. She started to throw them away, but in my state of perpetual hunger, I couldn't bear to see anything edible go to waste. "Just let them crumble up and stir them around in the pan a little longer," I advised from my rocking chair post. "I'll sprinkle them on something and eat them, I promise." Which I did. With gusto. At midnight. On top of pasta or guacamole or hummus. Or perhaps on top of all three mixed together. I can't clearly remember because it was dark, I was sleep-deprived, and foraging for food with a baby attached to one breast.

Mom's biggest success of all was "Southern Style Veggie Plate" night. Barbecue beans, smashed new potatoes with green onions and vegan Ranch dressing, zucchini stuffed with a fabulous mushroom filling, and a pasta salad. With a side of some of the vegan Mexican cornbread muffins I'd made and frozen when I'd had the strength to stand and stir (which seemed so long ago now), we were all happy eaters and having a lot of fun.

On the last full day of Mom's visit, I crawled into the fluffy guest bed with my baby and my laptop, handing Mom the former. I loaded snapshots from the hospital and our first few days onto Facebook and browsed the baby pictures my mom had uploaded with her clever captions written from Jackson's perspective. (She prides herself as being a Baby Interpreter.)

I've learned from Mom that conversations with babies are only as interesting as the adult's imagination. Giving Jackson an interesting voice became my new favorite pastime. Sometimes I chose a British accent for him with an edge of Winnie-the-Pooh. When he woke up, practically licking his lips with anticipation of his midnight snack, I'd have him say something adorably polite like "Pardon me, Mum, I was just thinking how lovely it would be to have a little smackerel of something warm, and perhaps a tad milk-ish." When he was fussy, I might bestow upon him a dramatic demanding voice, like a famous Will Ferrell character. "Ma! Meatloaf!!"

Clicking away at the computer made me feel a little like my old self for the first time in days. (I knew I was exhausted when simply logging on to Facebook felt overwhelming.) Just then, Mom walked in with a tray of what would be my last lunch made by her for a very long time. She outdid herself. The plate was beautifully arranged with a bowl of homemade hummus surrounded by pita chips, sliced strawberries and kiwis, three bean salad—tart from red wine vinegar and pepperoncinis balanced with sweet from a touch of sugar. I munched happily as I reveled in the unhurried time to respond to all the congratulations messages I'd received since Jackson was born.

The sun shone through the bedroom's gauzy white curtains, and life for that moment seemed pure and sweet and doable. I snapped a picture of myself with a plate of food in my lap, my laptop in front of me. Mom had placed sleeping Jackson near me, so I also snapped a picture of him dressed in a robin-egg-blue sleeping gown. He was all puffy kissable cheeks, leaning against a pillow. A bundle of sweet, sighing baby boy.

"You can do this, Rachel," Mom said as she softly stroked Jackson's little hand. "He is such a good-natured baby, and you are such a natural at being a mom."

"I think I *can* do this," I nodded, pushing down the feelings of doubt bubbling up inside.

I think I could see Mom swallowing a lump in her throat, but she was trying hard to sound peppy and positive. "I'm going to make a big batch of yellow pepper soup, a pot of refried beans, and blueberry oat bars. With that and all the meals you prepped for yourself, you probably won't need to make a whole meal until the Apocalypse ... or at least for a few more weeks. By then, you'll be ready to be back in the kitchen."

BECKY

I put on a brave front, but toward the end of my stay, I grew more concerned about Rachel. She was a natural at mothering, but she'd had a tough labor, was still weak and sore and exhausted. As a coach, Jared had to work late nights, overseeing high school practices and games, so he would not be around much to pitch in. I so wanted to stay longer, but my nonrefundable plane trip home was booked, and my husband was missing me back in Denver.

With both of us wiping stray tears from our eyes, Rachel and I said goodbye. I gave Jackson's downy-soft cheek one last peck before heading for the airport. Rachel smiled bravely through her tears, assuring me she'd be all right. I placed calls to my sister and my mother who lived about an hour away, asking if they could drop by and pitch in in my absence, which they were more than happy to do.

It was good to see Greg, the Love of My Life, again. But he could see immediately, when he looked in my eyes, that I was not fully present. I'd left a part of my anxious heart in Texas. The next day, I finally broke down and told him, "My daughter needs me. I need to be there. She wasn't even strong enough to complain about the mess I was making in the kitchen or care how I loaded her dishwasher. She's still *very* weak, Greg."

He hugged me and kissed my forehead and said, "Then go back to her."

I brushed the tears from my eyes. "Really?"

He smiled. "I've got a business trip coming up, so we'd be apart anyway. A girl needs her mama at times like this."

And that is how it came to be that within forty-eight hours of saying goodbye, I was back at my daughter's doorstep, suitcase in hand, gazing again into the shining dark eyes of my grandson. He grinned knowingly as soon as he saw me, as if he knew his Nonny couldn't possibly stay away long.

And stay I would, until I felt sure Rachel was ready to take over her own life again.

On the third day of my second visit, Rachel had the baby all nursed, swaddled, and asleep in the swing, then walked into the kitchen. The color had returned to her pretty face, her hair was done up in a cute curly 'do, and she was wearing lip gloss (the international female sign for "I'm feeling better"). Also, she walked without wincing. Then she automatically began re-rinsing and reloading the dishes I'd just put in the dishwasher.

I smiled. "Are you starting to feel a little irritated about things being out of place in your kitchen now?"

Rachel nodded.

And that is how we both knew it was time. Time for my daughter to fly solo as a new mom, to take charge of her own kitchen. And time for me to fly back to Denver, to my man, to make lots of creative, comfy messes in my own home again.

GOURMET RECIPES
FROM THE AISLES OF WALMART
Pecan Mushroom-Stuffed Zucchini

Delicious served alone as a vegetarian meal or as a side dish for any occasion. I like these so much I will munch on the leftovers cold, straight from the fridge! — Becky

Serves 4 – 6.

- ¼ cup olive oil
- ¼ cup butter or vegan margarine, such as Earth Balance
- 4 zucchini squashes, cut in half lengthwise with the middle cut or scooped out like a canoe (dice the scooped-out part for the stuffing)
- 8 ounces of mushrooms, any kind, diced (to yield 1½ to 2 cups)
- 2 cloves garlic, minced
- 2 pieces whole wheat bread made into crumbs (use your hands or a food processor to crumble)
- ½ cup pecans, chopped (walnuts are also great)
- ½ cup Parmesan cheese, divided
- ¾ teaspoon salt
- ½ teaspoon pepper
- 8 cherry or grape tomatoes, sliced for garnish
- fresh basil or oregano (enough for garnish)

Heat oven to 375˚. Put hollowed-out zucchini "boats" in a heat-proof rectangular pan, lightly salt and pepper them, and microwave for 6 minutes. In the meantime, heat oil and butter together in a skillet and add the reserved chopped zucchini, mushrooms, and garlic. Stir and cover, cooking over medium heat for about 5 minutes, so that juices accumulate and don't evaporate. When veggies are soft, translucent, and "juicy," toss in bread crumbs, ¼ cup Parmesan cheese, pecans, salt, and pepper. Stir. Turn off heat. Stuffing should be moist. (If dry, add a little more butter, oil, and/or water.)

Fill the "nuked" zucchini with stuffing, decorate with sliced tomatoes, cover pan with foil, and bake for 15 minutes. Remove from oven, uncover, and sprinkle with remaining ¼ cup Parmesan. Turn oven to broil, and put back in under the broiler, watching carefully until Parmesan starts to melt and tomatoes start to brown just a little. Garnish with fresh basil or oregano leaves.

Variation: Add cooked crumbled sausage for the omnivores in your family to make a complete meal-in-one.

- Vegetarian
- Vegan (use vegan margarine. Omit cheese or substitute with vegan Parmesan)
- Gluten free (use gluten-free bread)

Yellow Pepper Soup

I first tasted this soup on a trip to Florida, when a dear friend, Maxine Bland, served it up on her sunny back porch. It was February, but 70 degrees. I was not a big fan of soups back then, but it was love at first spoonful when I tasted this creamy dish. There's something in the combination of the roasted peppers and sweet potato that is simply . . . bliss on a spoon. —Becky

Serves 6 to 8.

4 yellow bell peppers, medium sized, seeded, rough chopped, and sautéed until just tender. (You can also roast them for a bit more flavor, peeling off the charred skin before seeding and chopping.)

1 cooked (baked, boiled, or nuked) sweet potato, peeled
    and rough-chopped

3 cups organic vegetable broth

½ onion, rough chopped

1 clove garlic, peeled

1 tablespoon maple syrup (or brown sugar)

¼ teaspoon fresh grated nutmeg

¾ teaspoon salt

¼ teaspoon pepper

6 tablespoons heavy cream or unsweetened vegan creamer
    (1 tablespoon for each of 6 bowls)

Into a blender, toss all the ingredients except the salt and pepper,
nutmeg, and cream. Blend until it's as smooth as you can get it and
transfer to a sauce pan. Cook over medium heat, stirring often,
about 10 to 15 minutes, until any raw onion or garlic taste is gone
and it is heated through. Add salt, pepper, and nutmeg; check for
seasonings and adjust to your liking. Serve in bowls, swirling 1
tablespoon heavy cream into each bowl, gently, using the tip of a
spoon just before serving.

  · *Vegetarian*
  · *Vegan (use unsweetened vegan creamer instead of cream)*
  · *Gluten free*

Blueberry-Raspberry Oat Bars

*These bars taste complex but are incredibly easy as you use the same
mix for the bottom crust as you do for the topping, and it's all blended
up in a food processor. Not too sweet and filled with oatmeal and
berries, these buttery bars will satisfy a sweet tooth without sending
you into sugar orbit. I've lost count of how many times I've made this
recipe and shared it with someone who asked for it! — Becky*

Serves 12 – 15, depending on how big you cut the bars.

1 cup butter

1 cup brown sugar or coconut sugar

1¾ cups flour

1 teaspoon salt

1½ cups oatmeal

½ cup chopped nuts (walnuts, pecans, almonds,
  or whatever nut you like)

1 cup fresh blueberries (or frozen blueberries, thawed,
  and juices drained)

1 cup fresh raspberries (or frozen raspberries, thawed,
  and juices drained)

Preheat oven to 375°. Put the first four ingredients into a food processor and pulse until crumbly. Add the oatmeal and nuts. Process just until blended. (You can also do this with a mixer or use clean hands for the job.) Press half of the mixture into a greased 9x13-inch pan. Spread berries over the crust and sprinkle with the remaining oatmeal mixture (like a crumb topping). Bake 25 minutes or until golden brown. Cool 10 minutes before cutting into bars.

If you have any leftovers (and this is a big IF), I've found they stay freshest when wrapped well and refrigerated: then nuke the portion you want to eat for a few seconds in the microwave.

- *Vegetarian*
- *Vegan (substitute butter with vegan margarine, such as Earth Balance, or coconut oil, or a combination of both)*
- *Gluten free (substitute flour with almond or oat flour and use gluten-free oats)*

Chapter 8

Lost in Mom Space

*Women need solitude
in order to find again
the true essence of themselves.*
Anne Morrow Lindbergh

RACHEL

"My cat has been staring at the door for ten minutes. He thinks if he keeps staring I'll open the door and it will lead him outside. Jackson is drooling and staring in fascination at my water bottle. He gets upset when it gets out of his eye line," I scribbled in my journal one morning. "I better get out of the house today before I too start staring blankly into the distance, my brain having turned to complete mom mush."

If you aren't careful, the first year of motherhood can be surprisingly isolating. Between multiple feedings, two to three naps, bath time, tummy time, and getting your child to bed, there's really not a lot of time left to socialize with people of the adult persuasion. And when getting out of the house means packing up and carrying around a diaper bag roughly twice the size and weight of the actual baby, you begin to wonder if it's even worth the trouble.

However, I was determined to at least try to interact with other mothers. So I hoisted my baby and super-sized diaper bag to attend a local MOPS (Mothers of Preschoolers) meeting. The coordinator closed the meeting with a prayer and then said, in her friendly Texas accent, "Bye! See y'all next time." I was sitting in the front row with forty other grown women, but I found myself holding both hands up next to my face, opening and closing my palms, saying "Bye Byeeee" in cute baby talk. The coordinator, a mom of three kids herself, laughed. "Rachel, sounds like you desperately need a Moms' Night Out."

Mommy Brain makes you indeed wonder, *Am I slowly getting dumber? Can I even make intelligible conversation with human beings who are taller than two feet anymore?*

I went to heat up a bowl of spicy butternut squash soup one afternoon. In some sort of out-of-body auto-pilot mode, I went to the fridge, grabbed the soup, poured a bowl, heated it in the microwave, and set it aside to cool. Then, without batting an eye, I grabbed another bowl, filled it with another serving of soup, microwaved it for 60 seconds, set it on the counter, looked down, and realized I had just served myself two warm bowls of creamy soup.

My mom has done things like this as long as I can remember. Growing up, it was almost habit, before putting my Hot Pocket in the microwave, to remove the cup of cold coffee or tea she had reheated and promptly forgotten about. Though my Granny insists that my mom was always a bit messy, ditzy, and forgetful, I now wondered if motherhood was actually the source of her scattered brain. As her daughter, I feared pregnancy and birth had activated in me some latent gene, the same one that made my mom absently throw her keys in the trash, or drive 20 miles an hour on the highway as cars zoom by her, completely unaware of her crawling speed.

In an attempt to stave off this gene, I'm learning to give myself a little time — sans baby — now and again. Without "Mommy's Time Out," as I call it, my brain just doesn't work right. It's like a computer on overload that begins working slow and wonky. All it needs is some time to shut down, and then it can go back to solving high functioning problems like *Just where did I put that pacifier?* or *On which side did I last nurse Jackson?*

The same principle applies to marriage. Jared and I learned early on how important it was to make date nights a priority, despite busy schedules and meager budgets.

After Jackson was born, we had to budget every penny we made, and there was nothing left over for fun. I'd stopped working, and hospital bills were starting to pile in. Still, by the time Jackson was two months old, Jared and I were in desperate need of a date night. We had plenty of grandparents pushing us to go out and leave the baby with them, but no money to go anywhere. So, instead, we got creative and turned our house into a romantic escape from parenting.

We called my dad and his wife, Pat, and asked if they could watch Jackson at their house for a few hours on a Saturday evening. They, of course, pounced at the opportunity. Before dropping Jackson off, we cleaned the house and cleared out all the baby items from the living room and kitchen. I looked at what we had in the pantry and the refrigerator and came up with a menu. With Jackson riding kangaroo-style in a baby wrap, I put Jared to work chopping vegetables while I baked, simmered, mixed, and taste-tested. Then we took turns getting showered and dressed up for our date. I put on a dress and heels for the first time since getting unpregnant. Just before we left the house to drop Jackson off at Grandpa and Grandma's, Jared set up a card table on our patio, covered it with a pretty table cloth, and turned on some classical music. On the way home, we splurged on a bottle of my favorite Pinot Noir.

Jared opened the door for me. "Welcome to La Villa de Randolph, the hottest (and only) vegan restaurant in town," he said. "I hear the food is delicious, but wait until you see the chef. I wonder if I could get a slice of her for dessert?" he flirted.

I grinned, throwing him my best come-hither look. "I don't know; I heard she already has a thing for her sous chef. Pretty racy stuff, I hear."

I dressed some Brussels sprouts, cut in half, with oil and balsamic vinegar, and a generous sprinkle of salt. Then I popped them into the oven to caramelize and roast, while I served us our first course: thinly sliced ribbons of carrot and broccoli marinated in a sweet and tangy vinaigrette. Jared poured the wine, and together, with beautiful strains of music taking the place of the cries of a fussy baby, we sat and talked (like grownups!) as we ate and enjoyed the pastoral view from our back-porch table for two.

Just as we finished the first course, we heard the timer in the kitchen go off. I pulled the Brussels sprouts out of the oven, which were now perfectly crispy and richly caramelized. I served them alongside mugs of stewed late-summer veggies with white beans. There was a chill in the air, but the creamy beans, new potatoes, and yellow squash, simmered in a chunky cherry tomato base, along with one another's company, kept us warm.

Later, as I sipped coffee and ate a pumpkin pretzel tart under the starry sky, I gazed at my husband, really seeing him for what felt like the first time in months. "Hey, we're talking! Like, really talking, and actually able to concentrate on what the other person is saying, in complete sentences!"

"It's nice," Jared said. "I've missed this."

"I've missed us," I replied.

～

As of this writing, Jackson is a year old. Recently, I had to leave him overnight for the first time. When I got home from my trip, I wrote this journal entry.

> He doesn't live and breathe me. We are not actually connected at the hip.
>
> I'm surprised. I'm humbled. I'm a little sad. I'm relieved.
>
> Before I left for two nights, I bathed Jackson and rubbed coconut oil through his hair and onto his legs. He has noticeable leg hair now and an ant bite on his ankle. He is no longer

silky soft, like a newborn. He is a little rougher these days, callused, and scraped from crawling and the inevitable falls that come with learning to walk. I can no longer protect him from the unavoidable wounds of the world.

Before I left, I nursed and rocked him and kissed his forehead and cried. *What will he do without me to comfort him?* Sure, his Mimi (Jared's mom) and his dad would be there to care for his basic needs and to entertain him. He adores them both, but it's me he reaches up for when he takes a hard tumble. I'm the only one who can nurse him when he's hungry. I wondered if he needed me too much for me to leave him overnight.

Months ago, when I booked the trip, I thought I'd be ready. I even thought maybe I would have weaned him by then. But I wasn't ready. I didn't want to go. I'd already made the commitment to my MOPS group to go to the International Convention with our team, and our church sponsors had paid most of my conference fees. I couldn't back out now.

That evening, while Jackson was groggy but still awake, I'd carefully handed him to Jared. He suddenly looked so big in his dinosaur pajama pants and matching T-shirt as I watched his daddy finish rocking him to sleep. Tears were pouring down my face now as I blew kisses and carefully closed his bedroom door.

I was a mess of distressing thoughts. *He won't understand. When he wakes up tomorrow and I'm gone, he won't understand. When he goes to bed tomorrow and I've still yet to come for him, he won't understand.*

I cried most of the hour-long ride to the conference, feeling like the worst mother that ever lived.

The next morning, I woke up with a clogged milk duct and was certain this was a sign I shouldn't have left. I called my mother-in-law, Rhonda, half-hoping she'd tell me to come home and that my son needed me.

She reported that Jackson had just woken up and was smiling and laughing. His giggling in the background confirmed she wasn't just trying to make me feel good. He was happy. She followed up with a series of pictures throughout the day of him splashing in the kiddie pool (assuring me he was wearing sunscreen and keeping his hat on), eating all of his lunch, and going down for a nap without a fuss.

I attended the general session and worship time that morning and couldn't hold back the tears. My friends were worried about me, knowing how anxious I had been about leaving my boy. They patted my back and assured me Jackson was fine.

I knew he was fine.

That's not why I was crying.

The tears were from relief.

I was off a hamster wheel I hadn't even realized I was on. It was like I had just stepped out of that little wheel and looked around, surprised that while I've been plodding along in my little world, a much bigger world was spinning all around me. For the first time in a year, my mind was free to think without worrying about my child, without the whisper of the baby monitor in the background or the clock ticking down the hour until I needed to pick him up from his grandparents' house.

My body was exhaling after a long, very long, almost twelve-months-long, inhale.

To my surprise and shock, I realized I was still a person, a single entity, with my own desires and feelings and needs. In a year, I had not allowed this person to feel or desire for more than a few guilt-ridden hours at a time.

But there she was in that big conference room, surrounded by thousands of other moms, exhaling, reclaiming her breath and her life.

I didn't cry the rest of the weekend, but I did skip out on one session to take a much needed nap. My roommates and friends

went out for a late dessert; I went to bed early for sweet uninterrupted sleep. How long had it been since I'd slept through the
night?

After seeing my sob session earlier, the other moms in my
group worried I would be lonesome in the hotel room all by
myself. They texted to make sure I was doing okay. Other than
my burgeoning boobs that had gone twenty-four hours without
the relief of nursing Jackson, I was more than fine. I was refilling
my exhausted body and parched soul. (As it turns out, an electric
portable breast pump is not nearly as efficient as a real baby.)

The following day I woke up feeling confident, alert, and
inspired. I felt like the old me, but even better. Motherhood has
made me stronger. I've felt needed in the deepest way, and I've
loved on a level I didn't know was possible. The way Jackson
desires my affection, attention, and love has been the most moving display of how I can love God as his child. To come to him
like a little child, to throw my hands up and say, "I want *you*. I
want to go where *you* go. I want to sit in *your* lap. I want to cry on
your shoulder." There are things about God that are hard to grasp
until you love a child. Then it all comes pouring in. I think of the
overwhelming love I feel for Jackson, my interest in every little
thing he does, my desire for him to experience deep love and joy,
my protective instincts that leap to shield him from any worldly
pain—and I realize afresh, in a whole new way, all of that is just
a fraction of the way God loves me.

Motherhood has changed almost everything in my life, yet
motherhood isn't all of me.

At the conference, I attended a session on "Making a Creative
Life" by author, blogger, mother of young children, and foodie
Shauna Niequist. I wondered how in the world she was making
room for everything in her life. That question echoed throughout
the room full of busy moms. She told us this:

"Creativity comes at an expense—something will not get

done. *But* creating will be worth it." She admitted her house wasn't perfectly clean and that she doesn't exercise much. When it comes to making time for her creative self, she is very disciplined. She makes appointments on her calendar, she arranges childcare, she lets the dishes sit, and she turns off the TV. I love this passage in her book *Cold Tangerines*.

> Do something creative every day, even if you work in a cubicle, even if you have a newborn, even if someone told you a long time ago that you're not an artist, or you can't sing, or you have nothing to say. Those people are bad people, and liars, and we hope they develop adult-onset acne really bad. Everyone has something to say. Everyone. Because everyone, every person was made by God, in the image of God. If he is a creator, and in fact he is, then we are creators, and no one, not a bad seventh-grade teacher or a harsh critic or a jealous competitor, can take that away.[4]

Or motherhood, I would add.

Jackson was fine while I was gone. He loves me and needs me, I know this. But he doesn't need me 24/7 anymore. He doesn't need me to spend my time away from him feeling guilty. He needs me to be me. And to be me, I need to have moments to hear myself think, to write, to read, to create. He needs me to have the courage to plunge into the little pockets of my soul that stir me toward Jesus, that make me smile, that make me feel like I've just jumped into a cool lake ... that refresh me. How else will he know to do the same for himself if I don't model this for him?

～

I returned from the trip and immediately signed Jackson up for a great Mother's Day Out program, something I knew I needed to do to finish writing this book but had stalled on and put off for months. I worried and fretted about leaving him there too, but my little guy walked right up to the nursery half-door, reached to open it, and then toddled off to play with the new toys and new friends.

He was happy. As I drove to a coffee shop, laptop in tow, I realized I was happy too. A few hours of creativity and a couple of lattes later, my arms were aching to hug my boy. He smiled and reached for me, so happy to be in my arms but not panicked or in distress from our time apart.

I think I can do this thing called motherhood, which is, let's face it, a long series of small "letting goes," inch by inch. Of course, with all the tears and sorrow of letting go, there is the surprising gift of newfound freedom of time added back into our lives, a remembering of who you are as a person, apart from all the mom roles you play.

I hold my sleeping little boy in my arms and accept this inevitable journey of life.

But still—I am in no hurry, as I savor all the stops along the way.

BECKY

This morning I am sitting on a beautiful patio in Arizona, having just enjoyed a leisurely morning of breakfasting and snuggling with my husband. We try to escape on an annual road trip together, during the last week of October and the first week of November, so we can act like honeymooners and be someplace green and sunny before the holidays hit. When we left Denver, the trees in our backyard were already heavy with snow. When we return, we will begin what I can only call "Johnson Thanksgiving Camp" because at least five family members are flying in for Thanksgiving (including Jared, Rachel, and Jackson!), and life will turn into a wonderful crazy chaos of cooking, playing, visiting, and loving on grandkids for seven days straight.

Perhaps one of the greatest compensations of growing older is that you get more days of sweet solitude handed to you on a silver platter—days that feel like an unexpected gift, or like a surprise breakfast in bed.

As I read Rachel's thoughts above, it makes me want to reach out and hug moms of little ones everywhere, to offer them big buckets of empathy. I am all too aware that for a young mother a day alone to do whatever she wants at any given moment may sound like science fiction or fantasy.

At fifty-something, I'm no longer young or wrinkle-free. My hair needs coloring; my chin needs plucking; my blood pressure needs monitoring. As my mom once told me, "After fifty, it's patch, patch, patch." I sometimes look wistfully at my beautiful young daughter and daughters-in-law and remember when ... sigh ... I looked like that. But because I married the first time at age seventeen and began producing babies right away (at my ten-year high school reunion I won the Most Likely to Populate the Planet Award), I don't think I had much time to savor the body and youth I'd been blessed with. I was too busy changing diapers, giving birth, and nursing children—and longing with every fiber of my being for a full night's sleep. An unhurried day alone, just for fun and pleasure, would remain a dream for what seemed like decades.

So I cherish the compensation of free time for the hassle and upkeep of growing older. Greg and I both work at home and are free to indulge in spontaneous flirting almost anytime we choose to do so. (And we choose to do so with surprisingly regularity. Sometimes we send email flirtations across the room, from my laptop perch on the couch to his computer in the lounge chair.) The sheer volume of togetherness has been such a gift to our marriage, and we know that the luxury of all this time together contributes to a relationship that feels so fun, close, and easy.

This summer we kept my five-year-old-grandson, Georgie, for ten days. On the third morning of being his full-time caretaker, I could not remember ever feeling so tired. I'd completely forgotten what it is like when you are no longer able to think two uninterrupted thoughts in a row, and even if you could do so, you'd be too tired to form any thoughts that made sense. Greg and I were just two ships passing in the hall, doing the "handoff" of Georgie, one of us resting up while the other one played with him. How did I ever have the emotional and physical fortitude to raise four small children so many years ago? I'd tell you if only I could remember. It's all a blur now.

As I sit on this upper-deck patio, looking forward to hours of writing (which still seems more play than work), iced coffee to my left, birds singing in the cloudless sky above, golfers chatting in the distance on an emerald course, I know these days are rare gifts to be treasured.

In this contemplative moment, I've decided there are three kinds of time a woman needs in her life to feel balanced and full. One is time with family and friends. That busy, hectic time feeds our social soul. The other is time apart with the love of our life. This passionate time feeds our sensual soul. Finally, there is time alone in which we can hear our own thoughts and, if we are blessed and quiet enough, also the voice of God speaking to our hearts. This solitary time feeds our spiritual soul. "Self-care is not selfish," writes my close friend Lucille Zimmerman, in her book, *Renewed*. "Without nurturing their own energy, passion, and health, and without setting limits on their own activity, women are useful to no one."[5]

I realize that young mothers do not always get the luxury of dividing and balancing their lives with all three kinds of time. At least not all in one week, maybe not even in a month. I remember one season when all four of my little ones got the chicken pox, one after another, and we were isolated for two months. There are times of sheer endurance in mothering.

From the vantage point of midlife, however, I would urge

moms everywhere to get creative as Rachel has done, and to gift yourself with whatever Kind of Time you are missing, especially when you feel off-kilter. Trade off babysitting with friends; give nearby grandparents or aunties the gift of time alone with your children; save pennies for a Mother's Day Out at least once a week. Then use that time for whatever you hear your heart whispering (or shouting) it needs: a fun lunch out with adults only, a hot date with your sweetie, or the company of your own delightful self.

When Greg and I are at home, where our life is so often centered on family, people, ministry, and work, I periodically find myself completely peopled out. I can't bring myself to answer one more phone call or email or to engage in one more session of listening with empathy to someone's problems. Usually Greg sees this look of stress in my eyes and asks, "Do you need a Becky Day?" This means I can leave the house and, without reporting my time or whereabouts, go and do anything that fills my soul at any given hour all day long. (I usually head to the Corner Bakery, the Tattered Cover bookstore, and the library, all conveniently located on one city block overlooking a pretty park.) Greg knows these times away are essential to my sense of balance and that in the long run everybody benefits when Becky is happy.

I come back refreshed and eager to see my husband who has braved the whole livelong day alone for my benefit. He always looks enormously relieved and happy to see me. Not long ago, after a day away, I came back around 5:00 p.m. and, refreshed and renewed, cheerfully whipped up a tasty dinner for two. Greg hadn't eaten lunch (if I am not there to feed him, he sometimes forgets to eat), and now famished, he looked up at me and then back at the plate of spicy catfish, oven-blistered potato slices, and fresh coleslaw and said, "You saved my life."

"Just by serving you dinner?" I asked.

"Yes," he said with deep conviction.

This good husband of mine is the most appreciative eater I've ever known. And because he is so grateful and kind, I spoil him rotten. Most evenings I cook a nice three-course dinner and bring our colorful, healthy, carefully arranged plates of delicious food to the living room, where we sit on our comfy couches and transform our coffee table—which rises on a spring—into a regular-height dining table. We'll eat and visit awhile and sometimes flip on the news or a nonviolent DVR'd show, like *American Pickers*. I created the rule of "no violence at dinner" when I discovered, to my shock, that my mild-mannered husband could happily and nonchalantly munch his dinner during *Braveheart's* beheadings or the *Band of Brothers* getting blown to bits. I, on the other hand, get woozy if a bird eats a worm on The Nature Channel.

But I digress. I was speaking about benefits of short absences from the daily grind. Aside from our own refreshment and renewal, these remind our families not to take us for granted, to be grateful for the little things we do for them, not the least of which is serving them regular nourishing meals—whether that is a simple bowl of chili and cornbread, a well-planned romantic dinner date on the porch, or a plate full of mouth-watering food to be lazily enjoyed on TV trays with a nice side of No Guilt.

I know Greg was exaggerating when he said, "You saved my life," but if you've ever been really hungry after a long day, and someone has greeted you with a hug and a hot meal, it can feel pretty close to life-saving. Perhaps it is no wonder that Jesus spoke of how when we feed others who are hungry—literally or figuratively—we are feeding him too. A cup of hot water or a steaming bowl of soup, served with love to our family and friends, in his name is, after all, no small thing.

Just remember that sometimes, at least now and then, we nurturers must also pause to feed our own hungry souls, to satisfy parched emotional and spiritual places with the cool water of unhurried time in God's presence, and be reminded of his great love.

He brought me to the banqueting house, and his banner over me was love.

Song of Solomon 2:4 KJV

ROMANTIC DINNER FOR TWO ON A BUDGET
Chili Lime Southern Style Catfish

I grew up in the South surrounded by lakes and fish fries, so I've eaten my share of catfish. This is how great catfish should taste. The coating is crisp without being heavy, and full of flavor!—Becky

Serves 2.

4 medium-sized catfish fillets

1 cup cornmeal

1 teaspoon grill seasoning (or ½ teaspoon salt, ¼ teaspoon
pepper, and ¼ teaspoon garlic powder)

1 teaspoon Tajins chili-lime spice (you can find this in the
Mexican food aisle of most grocers, or you can substitute
½ teaspoon ground red pepper, zest of one lime, and
½ teaspoon salt)

1 fresh lime, cut in half

sea salt

½ cup oil (I like a combination of coconut and olive oil
to equal about ¼ inch in your pan)

Heat oil in iron skillet on medium high until it is sizzling hot. Gently rinse fish fillets with fresh water and pat dry. Squeeze a little fresh lime juice over all the fillets, both sides. Then sprinkle both sides of the fillets with some good sea salt. Pour cornmeal on a plate or shallow wide bowl and mix in the grill seasoning and chili lime spice. Place fillets, one at a time, in cornmeal mixture, pressing the fish into it until it is lightly coated all over.

Using tongs, lay each fillet into the sizzling oil. Let cook until the bottom is golden brown and crisp, and then turn over and cook the other side. Don't crowd the pan too much; cook in batches if needed. When done, place on a paper-towel-lined plate and let any extra oil drain off. Test a bite to see if it needs more seasoning, and if so, sprinkle with additional Tajin or sea salt while it is still hot. Serve with tartar sauce, fresh lemon or lime, or cocktail sauce.

• *Gluten free*

Stewed Summer Veggies

I love to make this in the summer when Jared's uncle brings me bags full of vegetables from his organic garden. If you have a garden, or a generous gardening friend, this is the ultimate budget meal—almost free! Even though it's a warm soup, it's nice and light and isn't too filling for a romantic dinner for two under the stars. —Rachel

Serves 3–4.

- 1 tablespoon olive oil
- 1 large onion, diced
- 4 small potatoes, chopped into bite-size chunks
- 1 yellow squash (or zucchini), cut into bite-size chunks
- 3 cups of tomatoes (I use a combination of whole cherry tomatoes and chopped larger tomatoes)
- 1 tablespoon white-wine vinegar
- 3 stalks of kale, torn off the rib and into pieces (or 2 cups of baby spinach)
- 1 cup of water or vegetable broth
- 1 can of cannellini beans, drained and rinsed
- ¼ teaspoon seasoning salt (like Lawry's or Tony Chachere's Cajun seasoning)
- ¼ teaspoon smoked paprika
- salt and pepper to taste

Pour olive oil into a large tall-sided skillet or sauce pan and heat on medium. Add onions and a dash of salt and sauté for about 5 minutes. Add potatoes, squash, tomatoes, water or broth, and vinegar. Reduce heat to medium-low, cover, and cook for 30 minutes, stirring occasionally. Stir in kale and gently mash the cherry tomatoes so they release their juices. If it needs more liquid, you can add another cup of water or broth. Gently stir in the beans and season to taste with seasoning salt and smoked paprika (use just a pinch for a nice smoky flavor). Taste and adjust as needed, using salt, pepper, smoked paprika, and seasoning salt. Cook until greens are wilted.

- Vegan/vegetarian
- Gluten free

Oven-Blistered Potatoes

At least once a week, you'll find me tossing these babies in the oven to make a quick and easy side dish that tastes and looks complicated.
— Becky

Serves 2 – 4 people (depending on size of potatoes and appetites).

- 2 large or 3 medium Idaho potatoes, washed but not peeled, sliced thin (about ¼ inch or less)
- ¼ cup olive oil
- 2 tablespoons balsamic vinegar
- sea salt (fresh ground if you have it)
- 1 tablespoon chopped green onions or chives (optional)
- ¼ cup catsup, barbecue sauce, or ranch dressing for dipping (optional)

Place sliced potatoes in a shallow bowl and sprinkle with vinegar. Using clean hands, toss them around until they begin to soak up some of the vinegar. Add in the oil and do the same.

Lay "chips" on a big cookie sheet, spread apart and not touching each other. Lightly sprinkle them with sea salt. Broil about 4 inches from broiler on one side for 3 minutes or so, or until golden brown in spots. Remove from oven and turn over all the chips; sprinkle this side with more salt and put back under the broiler until the tops are golden brown. Remove from oven. The bottom side of the potatoes will have by now "blistered" and turned an even prettier shade of brown. Taste one as soon as they are cool to see if more salt may be needed. Garnish with chopped green onions or chives if you like. Serve with a side of ranch dressing, barbecue sauce, or catsup if desired.

Variations: Try it with different vinegars, like pomegranate balsamic or malt vinegar; or different salt combinations such as Cajun, lemon-pepper, or garlic.

- Vegan/vegetarian
- Gluten free

Broccoli Carrot Slaw

Ever wonder what to do with that big stem on the broccoli? This slaw uses every part of the broccoli to stretch your dollar but tastes and looks like it came out of a top chef's kitchen. —Rachel

Serves 2.

> 2 cups broccoli crowns and stems, thinly sliced into small flat ribbons
>
> 2 cups carrots, thinly sliced into small flat ribbons (a vegetable peeler works well for this)
>
> 4 tablespoons rice vinegar
>
> 2 tablespoons olive oil
>
> 2 tablespoons sugar
>
> 2 tablespoons sesame seeds
>
> 1 teaspoon sesame oil
>
> 1 teaspoon salt

Put all of the ingredients in a bowl and toss. Cover and refrigerate for at least 30 minutes to let the flavors mingle and the carrots and broccoli soften up. Can be served chilled or at room temperature.

- Vegan/vegetarian
- Gluten free

Chapter 9

"Whither Thou Beachest, I Will Beach"

We cook and eat to connect with family and friends
and with ancestors we never knew.
And through this baking bread together,
we come to know who we are and where we came from.

Bonny Wolf

RACHEL

Possibly the greatest material perk of marrying into the Randolph clan is access to Nana's Island.

Well, technically it's not really *Nana's* island, but if put to a vote by its residents, I'm pretty sure Nana would be crowned Queen of Little Gasparilla. For twenty years, Nana and Papa (Jared's maternal grandparents) have split their time between their lakefront home in Texas and an island condo off the coast of Placida, Florida.

Little Gasparilla is small, quaint, and has a way of transporting you back in time the moment you step on her shores. There are no stores and no cars. Islanders leave their vehicles, along with their worries, behind on the mainland. No doubt there's hassle involved to getting there. You have to park your car at Placida Harbor and then load all of your luggage, groceries, and beach gear into wheelbarrow-like carts as you board Captain Marshall's ferry to the island. To make coordinating trips to the mainland even more complicated, the ferry only runs a few times a day. But the reward for those inconveniences is more than worth it.

Once we are on that ferry, gliding across the bay, ocean breeze in our hair, the dolphins occasionally popping up around us, the magic begins. All eyes are locked on the dock ahead where all 4 feet and 11 inches of Nana is eagerly waiting to greet us, dressed in her flip-flops and linen sundress, waving wildly. "Hellooo! Hellooo! You're *here!*" she squeals.

The guys jump off the ferry to help the captain secure the boat to the dock. Nana hugs our necks, and one of her strapping grandsons picks her up for a little spin. We push our luggage-filled carts off the ferry and down the narrow dock. And as we near the end of the pier, we are transported to another world. Tree roots poke up through the shallow water, and purple orchids hang from the mangrove trees stretching up and across the dock. We push our carts down the shell path to our respective condos nestled in the trees. (When a lot of family comes, we usually rent a few other condos near Nana and Papa's place. The Randolphs, on the whole, travel in herds—no one wants to miss out on a moment of fun.)

As soon as we plop down our burdens, we open our suitcases and shimmy into our swimsuits. With the excitement of kids out of school, we walk down the boardwalk that winds through the sand dunes and tall beach grass (or as I view it now, "our wedding aisle") to soak up the last few rays of sun on the beach and to watch it set over the ocean, streaming ribbons of pink, orange, and rosy red in the sky and creating golden jewels of light on the water.

This summer, Jared and I carried our son down the boardwalk with us for the first time. It was the weekend of our fifth wedding anniversary. Five years earlier, I had walked down those very planks to say "I do" to the kindest and most loving man I'd ever met.

It stormed on our wedding day, all day, heavy torrential rains, lightning and thunder. Mom and I had to go to the mainland for my hair appointment at the local J.C. Penney salon, where blue-haired ladies were getting their weekly comb-outs, the only place open on a Sunday afternoon. On our return ferry ride, heavy winds and rain pelted us. We covered my up-do with a big plastic J.C. Penney shopping bag, trying desperately to save my curls from falling or frizzing.

Jared's cousins and best friend, Nick, greeted us at the dock with umbrellas and ponchos. "You look lovely," Nick said with a grin. Then, always a joker, he couldn't resist adding, "Does your dress match your plastic-bag veil?" I managed to crack a small smile and ducked under his umbrella. As we plodded through ankle-deep water, we looked at each other and I burst out laughing. "If I don't laugh, I'll cry."

At my condo doorstep, my smile turned to a pout. "Niiick," I whined, "it's raining on my wedding day."

"I know, Rach. That sucks."

"It really does. I need Jared."

To build anticipation for the wedding day, Jared and I hadn't seen or spoken to each other since the rehearsal dinner the evening before. Shortly after Nick left, my cell phone rang. It was Jared. "I'm sorry, I know we were trying not to talk until the wedding," he apologized, "but Nick said you needed me, and I kind of need you too."

"I'm glad you called," I sighed. "I don't know what to do. It's raining so hard."

"Everyone thinks we should move the wedding to the mainland," he gently suggested. "I know that's not what you want to hear, Rach, but if we start taxiing people over now, we can get everyone transported in time for the wedding."

"No," I interrupted with sudden clarity, "it's going to stop raining, and when it does, we will get married on the beach like we've always dreamed."

Long before Jared popped the question, when we were just dating, he and I sat against the sand dunes and dreamed about a simple beach wedding someday, with just family and a couple of friends. I'd been imagining this wedding scene for so long I could not envision an alternative. If the rain would just stop, everything could fall into place. I can be remarkably stubborn. "Jared, we're going to get married on the beach, even if we have to do it in the pouring rain." Jared knew by my tone that I was not joking, and the rest of my family knew that when I got "a bee in my bonnet" there would be no turning back. So everyone began sending pleading prayers heavenward, hoping they would somehow reach God's ear, even through all the dark clouds.

Forty-five minutes before the start of the wedding, the clouds parted, the sun came out, and the beach dried up. As soon as the rain stopped, everyone headed to the beach. Each family member had a little job to do to prepare the scene. (There are no wedding planners or special wedding packages on this little island. All hands would be on deck.) Nana and Aunt Kathy had been collecting big clamshells all summer, which Jared's little cousins, Maddy and Jana, quickly made into a wedding "aisle." My brothers set up tiki torches and carried the Communion table, complete with bread and wine, down to the water's edge. More guys set up the portable music, while womenfolk tied tulle ribbon along the boardwalk. Even the groom was down at the beach helping to rake the sand and clear the debris, brought in by the rain, thirty minutes before the wedding.

Meanwhile, I put on final touches of makeup while Mom recurled and pinned my hair, which had fallen flat and frizzy despite our shopping-bag shower cap. At that point, I would have walked down the aisle with an Afro. I just wanted to get married to Jared outside on the beach. That's all I wanted.

At the shoreline, my dad handed me off to Jared and joined the rest of the family standing behind us. Pastor Hugh Halter shared a few words of spiritual encouragement concerning marriage. I'm sure it was moving and inspiring, and if I had listened to it, it may have saved us from some early marital adjustments, but I didn't hear a word. Just behind Hugh, and throughout his entire message, two dolphins swam back and forth in the calm sea, staying just in front of the wedding party. Sorry, Hugh, but I think God wanted to assure me that indeed, he was there, blessing our marriage. The dolphins had my full attention.

I had been through a short, difficult marriage a few years before this moment. It ended in a heartbreaking divorce that I'd fought hard to prevent. Jared was a good man, a man of God who had kept incredible standards in order to one day honor his bride. I had struggled with feelings of unworthiness and feared that someday he would open his eyes and see this broken mess of a woman he was about to marry and run the opposite direction. Some close friends and church family, who had supported us while we dated, suddenly spoke disapproval when Jared proposed to a "divorcee." We'd been leading a Bible study at this church and had felt surrounded by grace, so this out-of-the-blue rejection stung terribly.

As we were reeling from that hurt, exactly one month before the wedding, Jared fell off a six-foot ladder and ended up in ICU with a serious brain injury. Needless to say, our engagement was a testing time. I spent more time on my knees in prayer in those six months than I'd probably spent in my whole life.

The dolphins, the clear sky, and the man standing in front of me, healthy and healed and apparently not running anywhere but into the sunset with his bride: it was all God's grace and mercy on this broken girl.

Now, here we were, five years later, walking across the very same spot we had said "I do" on that enchanting evening, but this time we each held onto one of our son's little hands, letting him feel the sand beneath his feet for the first time. We leaned over him and kissed each other. Again, I could feel God's benevolent smile of grace.

Of course, we'd be celebrating our romantic anniversary on this island with some company: my in-laws, brothers-in-law, grandparents-in-law, and one cousin. Oh, what's that you say? Your entire extended family doesn't join you for your anniversary celebrations? Well, how sad for you.

I kid.

Kind of.

We knew that when we chose to marry during the July Fourth weekend at the family beach compound, we would probably never get a solo vacation to the island on our actual anniversary. But let's be realistic: now that we are parents, we may never get a solo vacation again. There are some perks, indeed, to traveling with hordes of babysitters on standby.

We took turns snapping pictures of Jackson's first beach experience. One of my favorites is a silhouette of Jayce, Jared's youngest brother, and Jackson against the setting sun. Jayce is leaning down, holding Jackson up in the shallow water. Jackson is reaching down to touch the sparkling blue ripples with his fingertips. There's another image of Jackson, rapturous at the feel of sand between his dimpled fingers, his hands raised to the sun. The Randolph gang delighted in watching their first grandchild take delight in the pleasures of sun and sea and sand on this island that Jared and his brothers had loved since childhood.

And I was grateful to be a part of these loving, noisy, happy, enthusiastic people who make up my husband's family and who love our baby with joy and abandon.

BECKY

I read of my daughter's Florida island vacation with a mixture of delight and envy. Serendipitously, I was also on a beach vacation, also with my husband's family, but it would be a beach of a different color: mostly shades of gray. (No resemblance to the racy book of that same name.)

Because I adore my husband, I'm writing from inside our beach house in Neskowin, Oregon, where the ratio of rainy-cold-drizzly-foggy days to sunny days (even in July) is about a hundred to one. Greg loves this whole Oregon beach scene. The ocean shows off her waves by ferociously pounding and exploding against rocky shores, but it never calms or warms to the point where a human being can venture in for an actual swim. My Spanish blood craves sun, white sand, and a body of aqua water, which I can lazily float upon. It has taken some time and positive self-talk to adjust to my fair-skinned, red-headed Norwegian husband's version of a "beach vacation."

On the plus side, the fauna and flora here are truly magnificent. Because Oregon beach weather mimics a greenhouse, flowers grow in enormous profusion, many blossoms as big as dinner plates. The landscape is a verdant rain-forest green, which helps balance the lack of blue in the sky and the raindrops hitting your eyelashes.

Another positive: there are no worries about getting your body in shape, anticipating any kind of skin-to-sun exposure at the beach. You can have your cake and your unself-conscious beach strolls too. If you naively thought to bring a swimsuit, it will stay firmly tucked in your suitcase next to your sunglasses and suntan lotion. Top beachwear fashion in this neck of the woods consists of sweatpants paired with the alarming yellow and green Oregon Duck's hoodie. I am not sure if Oregonians as a lot are fair-headed and pale-skinned from their Scandinavian ancestry or because they've been water-logged and salt-bleached for a century, so that their skin takes on the hue of almost-white driftwood.

Finally, the great Northwest beaches are extremely conducive for Rip Van Winkle–worthy napping. I struggle to wake by 9:00 a.m. and pour a cup of coffee into my gullet, but I still find myself gazing dreamily toward the bed an hour later. There is a reason for the adorable coffee huts spaced every ten feet in this Land of the Overcast and Damp. One can only walk about ten paces before your eyelids turn to lead and your body collapses into the fetal napping position. Without regular ten-minute infusions of caffeine, the entire state would be useless, with no visible signs of life except the sounds of low snoring coming from couches and park benches.

The real reward of this place is the contented look in my husband's sea-blue eyes when he is here with his brother and sister and the smatterings of our collective kids and grandkids. Greg's mother and father came to this tiny seaside town of charming 1920s cottages before Greg, the youngest of their children, was born. It is one of those rare places that feels unchanged by time. Greg's father died in his fifties, his mother in her early sixties (though dementia following a stroke took her mind much earlier). Cigarettes robbed them both of many years they might have enjoyed. And so it is here that Greg reconnects with the best of times, with happy memories of his parents before they divorced when he was a young teen, when life was all it should be for a happy-natured red-headed little boy, Opie in his Mayberry. Greg's son, Troy, has adopted his father's love of Neskowin. He and his wife, Stephanie, have been talking about wanting to buy a cottage here someday. At the very least, we know Troy will continue the legacy of family vacations in this place with his own kids, and this thought warms Greg's heart and mine.

Though the mornings and afternoons are scheduled for personal laziness, I must come alive by five o'clock in the evening. It is every man for himself for breakfasts and lunches, but most evenings I cook dinners for the Johnson Clan, which usually numbers at least thirteen. Far from feeling like a kitchen martyr, I enjoy using my cooking skills to bless and nourish this family I've come to love. I've drawn on menus that I know people like and that serve a bunch on a budget: such as rich sour cream chicken enchiladas, sweet-'n'-spicy mini meatloaves, homemade spicy chicken tenders over crisp colorful salads. For a big lunch reunion for twenty-plus people, I made a vat of chicken-veggie tortilla soup and my famous buttery blueberry raspberry bars for dessert. Last night I made my mother's pineapple coconut cloud cake (just two ingredients in the cake) and took it outside on the porch to photograph for our food blog. When I looked up there was my grinning grandson, Georgie, peering through the window, licking his lips in anticipation.

I've got shrimp thawing for oriental rice bowls tonight. I'll make a giant bowl of jasmine rice with my handy-dandy rice cooker and will offer a variety of stir-fried veggies and meat to go on top, with a ladle of rich sweet-'n'-spicy lime Asian sauce and chopped almonds for garnish. Last night Greg's brother made perhaps the best spaghetti I've ever had, with black olives, fresh garlic, and chunks of Italian sausage. What would family vacations be without good meals around a huge table of overloaded paper plates, little kids sitting on laps, stories of old times passed around along with the salt and pepper and gravy? It has become something of a family tradition for Greg to tell about the time when, as a boy, he found a decomposing body washed up on another Oregon beach. Thankfully, he generally holds off on this story until after everyone has eaten their fill. He swears the macabre discovery did not traumatize him at all, that all he could think of was what a cool story he'd have to share with his buddies when school started again. If this had happened to me as a little girl, I'd still be in therapy and on megadoses of anti-anxiety meds.

It's been easy to cook for this gang, no special diets, no picky eaters, just grateful and hungry folks. I wonder, as I cook and try to feed so many people with various tastes, how Rachel and Jared were handling being vegans in a sea of carnivorous Randolphs on their extended family vacation.

RACHEL

After the whole clan finished posing for sunset pictures with Jackson on his first evening at the beach, we headed in for dinner. Nana and Rhonda had been on the island for a few days before we arrived and had cooked up a big batch of bean and vegetable soup in a beer broth to share with everyone. In a moving display of love for Jared and me, she left out the ham hock. You have to know the Randolphs to know *this* is love. After a long week of packing and preparing for this trip and a long day of multiple plane rides and long drives, I was exhausted and hungry. I'd had to travel alone with the baby, as Jared had to fly in from another city where he'd been coaching a baseball tournament that week. Jackson had a scary high fever the night before, and I'd hardly slept at all. I almost cried in my bowl of soup out of gratitude. I didn't have to add grocery shopping and cooking to my agenda on the first day at the beach. Papa made his special margaritas: a concoction of frozen limeade mix, ginger ale, tequila, and Gran Gala Orange Liqueur. We were officially on island time, simmering our dinner in beer and chasing it with margaritas. Aaaah.

Our second night, Jared and I took advantage of our eager and readily available "babysitters" to celebrate our five-year anniversary ... alone. We ferried over to the mainland, making ourselves at home at a casual little wine café with a live band playing relaxing music on the patio. We sipped Chardonnay (happy-hour special!) as we munched on a Mediterranean appetizer trio of hummus, olive tapenade, and roasted red peppers in garlic oil. We shared an eggplant and portobello wrap and a mixed green salad. I loved this meal so much, I made my own version as soon as we got home from vacation.

"I'm so glad we aren't at some stiff upscale restaurant," I told Jared. "Our wedding wasn't fancy, and our reception was casual. This is just so *us*."

"Do you have any idea how lucky I am?" Jared asked.

"Yeah, not only did you get to wear jeans to our anniversary dinner, but I'm a pretty cheap date too."

"Music to a man's ears."

Later we caught the ferry back to the island and walked along the moonlit beach, hand in hand. We stopped to sit against the sand dunes and reflect on all the good memories that had come to his family, and now to ours, from this little beach.

The evening of the fourth, Jared and I invited Nana and Papa to our condo for dinner. (Jim and Rhonda took Jayce to a local baseball game.) I made veggie fajitas, chunky guacamole, beans, and Mexican rice, and mixed up my own special margaritas with fresh squeezed limes, oranges, silver tequila, and simple syrup.

Nana and Papa, now in their early eighties, walked over to our condo, hand in hand. Papa's gait has slowed a bit after some painful surgery, but their enduring love is evident to all. I laughed as I saw Nana carrying her box of white Zin. Always prepared, that woman. If ever a party should break out at a moment's notice, rest assured, Nana will have the wine covered.

Without my trusty rice cooker, I accidentally undercooked the rice, but Nana, who can make the homeliest of people feel like a cover girl, talked up that rice with so many compliments that by the end of the night even I was convinced rice was meant to be crunchy. We talked and ate and laughed at the mess that was being made by Jackson, who was just learning to feed himself with a spoon.

Fresh organic blueberries were only three dollars a pint at the mainland grocery, so I stockpiled every time I went to the store that week. They were heavenly in my lemon blueberry crisp, a playoff of my mom's famous Lemon Blueberry Pie.

When the sky grew dark, we walked toward the ocean and watched fireworks on the boardwalk together. Jackson was mesmerized. "Boom, boom!" he said with each sparkling display.

Nana laughed and commented on just how smart and generally perfect he was in every way, as good Nanas tend to do with their grandchildren.

I don't know how many more years we'll have together on the island. As they get older, Nana and Papa may have to find a getaway that is closer to medical care, with paved, flat surfaces to walk on. But my stomach knots to think of visiting Nana's Island without them. I'm grateful for these moments while we have them close.

It is not a Randolph Vacation without a barbecue, so on our last night, the whole Randolph gang, along with several of Nana and Papa's dear island friends, gathered at the pool. My father-in-law, Jim, grilled burgers and brats. I asked Jim to leave some room on the grill for us so we could make veggie burgers and grilled avocados with corn, onion, and poblano pepper stuffing. He's grown accustomed to his daughter-in-law "sissifying" his "man grill" and hardly even cracks a joke about the veggies I toss on it anymore. I made a big tray of my favorite vegan oatmeal cranberry cookies. To my delight, the tray was empty when I went to collect my dish from the buffet. As we started to walk out, a friend of Nana's slipped me his business card. "Will you send me the recipe for those burgers and cookies when you get a chance?" he asked. I've never felt so flattered by a man in his seventies.

By the time we'd said our goodbyes and were heading to our respective homes, we'd spent nine days on a remote island with an eleven-month old baby and my in-laws. This probably sounds like fodder for an episode of *Survivor* to most. And trust me, throwing this Type-A, routine-loving, quiet girl off schedule and into the mix with her husband's family, all of whom talk fast, loud, and over one another, called upon my slow-breathing skills now and again. Every Randolph conversation is an intense debate or an exciting story. I'm still adjusting to the sheer volume of it all. But over the years I've come to appreciate that the same passion they bring when defending a call in a football game is the same abundance of passion and love they feel for their family.

Nana and Papa just celebrated their sixtieth wedding anniversary. Both of their adult kids have been happily married for more than twenty-five years. They do not let go of each other, no matter what challenges life brings. Love is nourished and cherished and celebrated at every opportunity. It warms my heart to know that this man I married was raised with a legacy of faith and faithfulness and that, come what may, he will never let go of me either.

BECKY

Back in the mist and fog of our "beach house," everyone helps with cleanup after dinner. While the rest of the gang plays penny family poker, I always take my Georgie for meandering walks to the beach and back. Georgie is all boy on our walks. He's never without a stick, which he waves as he jumps and twists and turns, a Ninja fighting invisible enemies — stopping now and again to hit a tree or a rock for noisy good measure. Greg's grand-niece, Jenna, age six, has been the perfect playmate for Georgie this week, showing him how to play hopscotch in the sand and listening to audio books on my Nook, one after another. But she is all girl, concerned each morning about which of her cute outfits to wear. She went on a walk with us one evening and, observing Georgie's energy, finally asked him flatly, "Georgie, are you hopped up on veggies or Mountain Dew?" I tried to explain to Jenna that Georgie was simply "hopped up" on boy juice made mostly of slugs and snails and puppy-dog tails. Or as it has been said, "A boy is noise with dirt on it."

Of late Georgie has been into Johnny Cash songs, which he calls "powerful music." Yesterday, I watched him sing along to some sad, lonesome Cash ballad, his little cowboy hat bobbing, his brows creased seriously, as he belted out, "I hung my head," and then some verse about shooting somebody with "my brother's rifle." There's not a thing wrong with my life, but after two Johnny Cash songs I start feeling chemically depressed. So we switched the radio to an upbeat country song he likes with lyrics about "driving with my red top down" and "I wanna do right but not right now." Not exactly Kindermusik, but at least we got our toes tapping.

Georgie and his mom, Julie, had to leave to drive home to Seattle yesterday, and the look on Georgie's face broke my heart. Tears standing in his eyes, he sadly let his Poppy carry him to the car and buckle him in before solemnly asking his mom to put in a Johnny Cash CD. Apparently this was a Man in Black moment. Georgie's dad, my son Zach, is an Alaskan fisherman and often away for months at a time. There have been too many long separations in that little boy's life. Julie called later and told me Georgie shed silent tears off and on all the way home, missing the beach and missing this big, happy blended family of ours. Oh, what I would give for Georgie never to have to say another goodbye, to never shed another tear, for his life to be always "hopped up" on happiness.

It is moments like this when I want to say, "Forget this modern life where families are all scattered across the country!" These are the days when I wish our humongous family with multi-generations all lived in one giant yellow two-story frame house. The kind where we could shout, "Goodnight, John-Boy," before turning out the lights and snuggling under home-stitched quilts. Where there would always be a bevy of aunts, grandmas, and babies at the kitchen table, shelling out stories alongside bowls of fresh peas, and a field full of men and boys harvesting something hearty from the land. The kind of life where my grandkids could wander in the kitchen at any time to sit a spell and get a hug and a cookie from their Nonny or go outside to hit a baseball with their Poppy.

Then I remember that as much as I adore our huge family, I also love the quiet cozy "couple-only" times in my loving marriage. I too know the heartache of divorce, of fighting a long painful battle trying to keep love alive. A good marriage is not a given in this life, and if you have one, you are blessed beyond belief. Your love, together, deserves to be nourished, cherished, and celebrated.

I am incredibly thankful that Rach found her Jared soon after I found my Greg. We often tease that Jared and Greg have to be related in some way; they have so many similar interests and the same laidback, patient personalities and passionate, protective, faithful love for us, their wives.

Greg woke me this morning, after his return from a long early morning walk in search of sand dollars. I was still being pulled by the strong tide of sleepiness when he snuggled back in bed beside me and said, "I was walking on the beach, thinking of you, Becky. And how happy I am, how happy you've made me." My husband's kind presence eases the pain of my grandson's departure as I lay in his arms, soaking in his love, like a balm.

⁓

Greg's sister Gail and I worked side by side in the kitchen at breakfast time. I watched as she made her famous scrambled eggs for Jenna, using a dollop of mayo in the egg mixture. "It makes them taste richer," she said. We chatted about Gail and Greg's mother, Shirley, and Gail remembered that her mom used to pinch off a piece of butter and eat it whenever she opened a new stick. "Mom only did it when the stick was new. It was like a little ritual. She'd also take the occasional swig of vinegar — straight out of the bottle!"

"Are you sure it was vinegar and not vodka?" I teased.

Gail laughed and assured me the bottle held nothing stronger than apple cider vinegar. I treasure these glimpses of Greg's mother in the kitchen and put them together with the other memories Greg's shared of her: doing the Charleston in the living room, delighting in her young grandsons, laughing and joking while playing bridge, listening for hours to records of Sinatra, Dean, and Sammy. Every year that passes I get to know more of Greg's family and his history, until they now seem a part of me. Greg's seen my nieces grow from toddlers to pre-teens and witnessed my parents' fiftieth anniversary. Together we have seen major milestones in our children's lives: five college graduations, three weddings, one marathon, and the birth of four grandsons and the adoption of a fifth. We've also seen our adult kids walk through grief and loss, job loss and gains, two brain injuries (both are now fine), two blood clots, three surgeries, one shattered ankle, and a collapsed lung. We've vacationed with most of our kids and grandkids. Like all big families, we've had our share of relationship struggles, but we always find our way back to forgiveness and love. The best of times and the worst of times have more than blended us; they've bonded us.

My daughter is experiencing this union of families as well, and even more so now with the arrival of Jackson. I can see from Rachel's emails and phone calls and the pictures she's posting on Facebook that Jared's family, along with their beloved island, are weaving themselves into the warp and woof of Rachel's heart.

Even the Northwestern fog and mist is growing on me, or perhaps growing within me, in the heart-place where all that my husband treasures are becoming my riches too.

Marriage is much more than two people joining lives. It is two histories combining, two stories merging, two families creating new legacies together. It is the ultimate potluck of people: surprising, eclectic, quirky, and—if you are lucky—something altogether quite wonderful.

One evening, soon after we returned from vacation, I put on a CD and, while Sinatra crooned "Fly Me to the Moon," I lit the stove, put on a fresh apron, and began to cook supper. I reached in the fridge to open a new stick of butter, then paused, ate a little pinch of the corner and smiled.

> Whither thou goest, I will go; and where thou lodgest, I will lodge: thy people shall be my people, and thy God my God.

Ruth 1:16 KJV

BEACHIN' RECIPES
Tortilla Soup

I adore this soup, especially when I need to serve a crowd. People love adding their own "fixin's" (which I put out on a buffet), and by doing so, you create a one-bowl wonder. Add some cornbread, and dinner for a dozen is done. — Becky

Serves 10–12.

1 seeded red bell pepper

½ red onion

3 cloves garlic

2 teaspoons poultry seasoning

2 teaspoons cumin

1 tablespoon brown sugar

1 to 2 chipotle peppers in adobo sauce (medium to hot heat level), available in small cans in Mexican and Spanish food section of market.*

1 28-ounce can fire roasted crushed tomatoes, divided in half

4 cups chicken or vegetable broth (divided 1 and 3)

3 to 4 cups deli roasted chicken, pulled off bone and diced or shredded

---

*I keep the leftover Chipotles in Adobo Sauce in a small Ziploc bag in the freezer and break off what I need to add depth of flavor and heat to other Mexican dishes.

1 cup frozen corn

1 zucchini, diced

steak or grill seasoning (or salt and pepper), to taste

¼ cup barbecue sauce

½ cup heavy cream (optional)

Topping Options: crushed tortilla chips, grated cheese, chopped
green onions, diced avocados, sour cream or Greek yogurt,
wedges of fresh lime, cilantro

In a blender or food processor put the first seven ingredients (bell
pepper through chipotles), half of the crushed tomatoes, and one
cup of broth. Blend well. Pour this mixture into a big soup pot
and add the rest of the crushed tomatoes and broth. To this, add
chicken, frozen corn, and zucchini. Simmer over medium heat
until zucchini is tender and soup is heated through. Season with
steak or grill seasoning (or salt and pepper) to taste. To make a
creamier soup, add ½ cup of cream.

To serve, put a handful of crushed tortilla chips in the bottom
of each soup bowl. Carefully ladle on soup, and then top with your
choice of toppings.

- *Vegetarian (use vegetable broth, and pinto, ranch-style,
  or black beans in place of chicken)*
- *Vegan (follow steps above and omit cheese and cream)*
- *Gluten free*

Pineapple Coconut Cloud Cake

*My mother, Ruthie, introduced this light-as-a-feather cake to our
family a few years ago to rave reviews. When we discovered the cake
itself has two ingredients, needs no mixer, and is low in fat and
calories, we all begged for the recipe. — Becky*

Serves 12.

1 angel food cake mix

1 20-ounce can crushed pineapple

3 cups whipped topping*

½ cup shredded coconut for sprinkling on top

Optional: toasted, sliced almonds

Preheat oven to 350°. In a big bowl, stir or whisk together one box of angel food cake mix and a large can of crushed pineapple with juice. Pour into a 9x13-inch ungreased pan. Bake until golden brown, 25 to 30 minutes.

To cool, turn the cake upside down, propped up on 4 cans or cups of equal height, at corners. When completely cool, frost cake with whipped cream or topping, garnish with flaked coconut and optional toasted sliced almonds. Serve and enjoy. Keep in fridge, covered.

· Vegetarian

Grilled Stuffed Avocados

Serve these at your next barbecue with Mexican rice and beans and no one will even miss the meat. —Rachel

Serves 2 entrees (4 appetizers).

Stuffed Avocados

2 ripe but firm avocados, cut in half lengthwise and pitted

2 ears of corn with husks, soaked for 30 minutes and silks removed;
   pull husks back but don't remove from cob

1 poblano pepper

½ red onion, sliced into ½ inch thick rings

---

* My mom loves Dream Whip, which she makes from a box. I'm a real cow's whipping cream kind of a girl. Cool Whip is the most convenient for occasions when there may not be a mixer handy. Coconut-milk whipping cream is also great—use the thick cream that floats from the top of two cans of full fat refrigerated coconut milk and whip, and then sweeten just as you do whipping cream with vanilla and sugar.

2 tablespoons canola oil

1 teaspoon kosher salt

juice of ½ a lime (about 1 tablespoon)

Cilantro Lime Sour Cream Sauce

¼ cup vegan or regular sour cream

¼ cup cilantro

½ tablespoon lime juice

¼ teaspoon salt

1 clove garlic

Light coals for charcoal grill. You want the coals to be all white and no longer flaming when ready. (You can also use a gas grill on medium-low flames.)

In a blender or food processor, blend all ingredients for the cilantro lime sour cream sauce. Set aside.

Mix canola oil, salt, and lime in a small bowl. Brush corn with canola oil mixture and pull husks back up around kernels. Brush onions with canola oil mixture. Put corn, onions, and poblano pepper (left whole) on the grill. Apply canola mixture with a grill brush as they cook and turn veggies so they cook evenly on all sides. When poblano is charred on all sides, remove it and put it in a bowl covered with plastic wrap for a few minutes to loosen the skin. Remove the skins with a wet paper towel. Grill onions and corn for 15–20 minutes until they are cooked through and lightly charred. Cut corn off the cob; dice onions and poblanos about the same size as corn kernels. Toss together in a bowl.

Brush avocados with canola mixture and grill flesh side down for 3–4 minutes. Ideally, you'll get nice grill marks across the avocado. Nestle the grilled avocados in a bed of Mexican rice, top with corn, onion, and poblano mixture, and drizzle with cilantro sour cream sauce. Serve with a side of black beans for a complete meal or as a healthy side dish or appetizer.

· *Vegan/vegetarian*
· *Gluten free*

Chapter 10

Family Bonding in the Kitchen

*Cooking with kids is not just about ingredients,
recipes, and cooking. It's about harnessing imagination,
empowerment, and creativity.*

Guy Fieri

BECKY

I know I've spoken in glowing terms of my husband, Greg, in this book. So what I'm about to tell you may come as a shock. Greg is not perfect. In fact, though he's a wonderfully talented businessman, husband, and family man, and holds his own on the golf course, he is so bereft of cooking skills that I shudder to think of how he will survive if something ever happens to me. Unless someone comes to his rescue in the kitchen, he will subsist on Fritos, potato chips, and toast, washed down with a glass of cold milk. (*Lord, please grant me a long life so my husband has a chance of having one too.*)

Though Greg doesn't cook, at least not with anything other than an upright toaster or the microwave to reheat leftovers, he is generous with helping me clean up after I've cooked dinner. Since, after I whip up a fabulous meal, the kitchen looks like a hyperactive child just opened the fridge and started throwing everything in it onto every available surface, this is no small gesture of love on his part. There is, however, one thing Greg has done in an attempt to "help me in the kitchen" that has brought me within inches of insanity.

The first time he did it, I came unglued, but apparently not memorably enough to prevent him from doing the same thing a month later. Here, in horrid detail, are Greg's crimes against food. The first offense occurred one night after I had spent hours making a beautiful pan of spinach manicotti with a chunky, rich homemade marinara. I swaddled the dish like a baby to keep it warm as we drove to a church leadership meeting. I carefully placed the pan on a counter and turned my back for a mere minute. When I turned around, Greg was holding a knife and CHEER-FULLY cutting the manicotti into — and this pains me to say it — *SQUARES*! He treated my dish like some cheap Stouffer's lasagna instead of following the precious outline of the tubular pasta. I died a thousand deaths, but did not scream or yell. I just pointedly said, "Greg, please don't ever come anywhere near my manicotti with a knife again."

A month later, I made sour cream chicken enchiladas. Another long labor of love. Beautiful they were. Lovely little corn tortilla bundles stuffed with chicken and three kinds of cheese, dressed with silky white sour cream and green chili sauce. After dinner, there was a whole pan of them left over, which I planned to cover with plastic and tuck away in the fridge. But Greg said he would put away the food and clean up the kitchen for me, a sweet and generous offer. The next day I discovered The Slasher had returned. I found my gorgeous enchiladas, cut into small squares, like *brownies*, and stacked on top of each other in a tall Tupper-ware container. If you're a foodie, I need not tell you how my heart flopped onto the floor. Your heart is already there in empathy. If you are a noncooking guy like Greg, you're probably thinking, *So what's the big deal?*

I think I finally got through to him when I held up a knife and said, "Anything that comes naturally formed in the shape of a cylinder or tube, should not be hacked upon. It should stay in the same shape in which it was originally created." He nodded in full understanding.

After almost a decade together, I can see that Greg is never going to make an omelet or toss a salad or bake a muffin. He may cook a steak on the grill, but trust me, you would not want to eat it.

Thankfully, all of my adult children love to cook. In fact, Rachel's youngest brother, Gabe, would rather come over and cook a gourmet meal together than go out to eat. We chop and sauté with ease as we laugh and chat. He is as comfortable in a kitchen as he is on a ski slope. I don't think I fully embraced a deep love of home-cooking until my midforties, when I entered a new life space and my kitchen became something of an art studio-sanctuary to my soul. I can't say for sure why my four extremely different grown children all came to know their way around a saucepan, since my presence in the kitchen has an uneven history. I am just so glad they did, because working elbow to elbow in the kitchen with my kids is currently one of my greatest joys.

Now that I have five grandsons, I am having an absolute blast creating great food memories with the next generation.

Over the years, I've collected cups decorated with each of the boys' favorite movie or toy heroes, and they know just where to go and get their "fishy plates" (plates with divided trays, shaped like a fish, with "tails" that the boys can hold as they fill their plates). It's amazing how quickly children will adjust to and enjoy their traditions and how they do not take kindly to you messing them up. (A word to the wise: once you designate a "special cup" to one grandchild, do not accidentally give said cup to a visitor, a sibling, or a cousin. You *will* hear about. And it will not be pretty.)

Nate, my first grandson, has been a bit of a picky eater, but like his Uncle Jared, what he likes, he likes a lot and does not tire of eating: fruit, kidney beans, avocados, and his favorite thing in the world: cheese. I bought a special grater that grates fluffy haystacks of what I called "hairy cheese," that he would gobble up with his fingers in a flurry of delight. He loves to help make "pizza" together, which is a piece of naan bread (flat bread) that I grill on a skillet, then let Nate cover with "hairy cheese" (which melts on contact with the hot bread), and dot it with avocado.

Remember my heartfelt wish that my grandson Georgie would have fewer tough goodbyes in his life? Within two weeks of writing that paragraph, Georgie flew all by himself from his home in Seattle to our home in Denver for Thanksgiving. ("What was your favorite part of the trip?" I asked him after the flight attendant delivered him to my waiting arms. "Being brave," he said, grinning from ear to ear.) Through an unexpected series of circumstances, Georgie never had to say the dreaded goodbyes to me and his beloved Poppy, and never had to return to Seattle.

His mother, Julie, decided to relocate to Denver, where jobs in her field are more plentiful, and they are living with us for the time being. (Zach is away on another long season of winter crabbing.) Needless to say, I'm in Nonny heaven, cherishing this gift of unhurried time together.

Georgie, who has been through so many changes in his young life, adores rituals and routines. Every morning he eats the same thing; a bowl of what he calls, "Frosted Wini-Meats." (I think the way he says it is so cute, I don't have the heart to correct him.) After he attends kindergarten, mere blocks from our house, he likes to have a snack we call "palm trees," which is a piece of string cheese, and a peeled clementine orange, opened slightly, like leaves and plopped atop the cheese.

Every evening, after Georgie and his Poppy have their "wrestling time," Georgie can count on getting to "cook with Nonny." He drags an old red stepping stool up to the counter and awaits his orders. He peels potatoes and carrots like a pro now, can tear lettuce into a beautiful salad, but most of all he loves to stir anything. One night, a few weeks ago, I let him help me mix up a pumpkin pie (so easy for kids), and then I let him stand by the mixer while he watched me make whipped cream, his eyes widening as the cream formed into silky peaks. I let him lick the beater, and he literally rolled his eyes to heaven and "MMMmmmed" until that beater gleamed, not a speck of cream left behind.

He was all smiles, later, as we sat at the kitchen table, eating our pumpkin pie smothered in fresh whipped cream. "Nonny, what day is it?"

"It's Wednesday, Georgie."

"Do you always make pie on Wednesdays?" he asked hopefully, his brown eyes shining.

"Would you like that?"

"Yes!"

"Then Wednesdays will be pie days."

And so Georgie and I bake a pie together every Wednesday. Last week it was a fresh blueberry. I can't wait to introduce him to Aunt Etta's chocolate pie this week.

Thanksgiving is always a huge affair, and I often cook for twenty to thirty. It is exhausting, but the memories are always worth it. I have a picture I love of one of my grandsons when he was tiny, maybe a year old. He was wearing a little button-up flannel shirt and impossibly small jeans, sitting on my kitchen counter, his bare feet in the sink. I am in an apron at his side, laughing as I watch him joyously pick turkey meat off the carcass, and eat it with glee, giving a suspicious sideways glance to anyone who might dare to stop him.

Another thing grandkids love to do at our house is have a Toothpick Picnic. I found and purchased two colorful plastic plates with a dozen indentions for deviled eggs. When the boys got old enough to be trusted with a toothpick, I'd put little bits of food in each indention—a square of cheese, a grape, kidney beans —and let the boys stab them with toothpicks and eat them carefully. Titus, Nate's little brother, would just about hyperventilate when one of the indentions became empty, after he ate the piece of food occupying the space. His mouth would be bulging with the food as he frantically pointed to the indention saying, "More!" So I'd have to sit by him and continually fill the empty spots to avoid a kitchen-table meltdown. Nonnys, as all grandkids know, will do anything to keep their grandchildren from being upset. I find a way to say three yes's to avoid one no. If they want to use a sharp knife, for example, I'll happily offer three other safe, fun suggestions (child scissors? plastic knife? popsicle stick?) in its place, carefully avoiding the *no* word at all costs.

As Jackson grew big enough to enjoy real food, while he was still breastfeeding, Rachel supplied him with only the healthiest of foods. One of my favorite "first food" pictures is of Jackson with his little neck up-stretched, a smile so big his eyes have almost disappeared, gripping two fistfuls of kale, rather like a cartoon baby Tyrannosaurus. Remember how worried I was that Jackson would be small, perhaps of delicate constitution, since Rachel was so little in her pregnancy? As soon as he was born, Jackson was already struggling to hold his own head up. Then in no time it seemed, he was trying to stand and jump on our laps as we held his little arms. As soon as he could crawl, then stand while leaning, he took to moving furniture around the house as his playtime activity, something I've never seen a child do. His hair had turned blond but still had that fresh haircut look at all times. Wearing just his diaper as he moved chairs, barstools, and anything that wasn't nailed down, he looked for all the world like a Pro Baby Wrestler. All he needed was barbells and a wide rhinestone studded belt. While most mothers have to pick up toys after a day of letting the baby play in the living room, Rachel would spend a few minutes every evening putting the furniture back in place.

Jackson also loved all things related to food, and while on a visit to our home, when he was about nine months old, he would do a stunningly choreographed Happy High Chair Dance when first given his meal. His arms would go up, feet out, all four limbs swinging and bouncing while his head nodded in simultaneous and delightful approval. Such an appreciative dinner guest.

Last week Rach sent me a video of Jackson drinking miso soup from a bowl. His entire face disappeared into the bowl as he slurped noisily, only pausing to breathe and look at his mom to voice a sincere, low "Mmmmm ... mmmmm" before he dived back into the bowl for more goodness, again and again. I may have done the very same thing when I first tried miso soup about four years ago. I had been feeling poorly, and it was the first thing I tried when my stomach settled. It tasted so good, like liquid butter. I also could not stop audible "mmmms" of satisfaction.

RACHEL

Besides rearranging furniture, some of Jackson's other favorite "toys" are the rice maker, a four-cup coffeemaker (without the glass pot), the salad spinner, and of course the universal childhood favorite, pots and pans. At fifteen months old, he likes to drag his coffeemaker around by the cord from room to room, like a puppy on a leash, and assemble and disassemble the rice maker and salad spinner ... over and over and over again. He opens up the great big drawer near my oven with every pot, pan, and lid I own and proceeds to take out every single one. He's gotten surprisingly good at matching the right lid with the right pot.

Cooking with him around is like cooking on an obstacle course. Chop the onions with a twenty-pound kid hanging on your leg. Drag said kid along as you locate the pan you need (it could have "migrated" anywhere in the house). Hop over an appliance while balancing a cutting board full of diced onions on your way from the island to the stove top. Sauté the onions while dodging lids skidding across the floor at your feet. And that's just step one. I'm pretty sure I burn all my calories while cooking, which is convenient for me, since I haven't stepped into a gym in more than a year.

I thought about putting locks on the cabinets. I even emptied a cabinet and filled it with various kitchen items just for Jackson. I showed him his very own space with much enthusiasm. He was bored with it in minutes. In the end, I decided to leave the cabinets unlocked, simply moving anything too delicate out of his reach. Yes, my kitchen gets turned upside down with every meal I cook. Yes, all of my Tupperware and pots and pans have been glided across my dirty floors. But cooking makes me happy, and if giving him reign over my cabinets is what he needs to stay in his happy place while I am in my happy place, then may the innards of my cabinets overfloweth onto my floors. Casseroles and apple crisps need baking.

For Jackson's first birthday, I splurged on a FunPod, a rather pricey European contraption that safely elevates him to counter height. It looks like a chair with four walls and an adjustable platform.

Best. Purchase. Ever.

Not only does this contraption keep him out of my pots and pans (for a little while at least), but it buys me even more time in the kitchen. This makes me happy. While I cook, I hand him bits and pieces of ingredients to play with and taste. One day, while I was tearing up kale leaves to add to a stew, I gave Jackson a few leaves to occupy him. I was busily cooking at the stove when I turned around and saw him in his FunPod methodically tearing the leaves into bite-sized pieces and putting them in a bowl. My boy was making his first salad. It is my proudest parenting moment thus far.

He watches me in the kitchen, and he's learning — about more than just food. He uses all his senses "helping" me cook. He touches different textures as he reaches into a gooey batter or crumbles up stale bread. He smells the difference between sweet lavender sugar cookies baking, warm pumpkin spice cobbler bubbling, and enticing garlic bread crisping under the broiler. He sees steam rising from the boiling pasta water and makes the connection. "Awwwt" (hot), he tells me, pointing to the steam. He sees deep shades of purple in an eggplant cut open to reveal the contrast of its white spongy flesh. No box of colors can capture that or the shades of dark olive green on the tough bumpy skin of an avocado and its soft green creamy insides. He bites into an unpeeled banana. It's bitter and tough. He learns. The outside is "yucky, yucky," but, "mmmm," the inside is sweet and easy to chew.

Letting young kids in the kitchen doubles both your cooking and cleaning time, but it's not just about getting food on the table quickly. It's a time to teach and to be taught. To be taught to slow down. To pay attention to details as you point out colors and shapes and make taste-memories with each other. Like caramelizing onions, cooking with kids takes patience and tenderness. A bitter raw onion cooked low and slow turns so sweet you could puree it and eat as jam on your morning toast. Patience is sweetly rewarded in the kitchen.

Jackson's favorite meal is a veggie bowl. I sauté mushrooms and garlic in a little olive oil, then add kale (torn into tiny pieces) and a little vegetable stock and slowly simmer it until the kale is soft. At the last minute, I add kidney beans and a pinch of smoked paprika and salt. I never skimp on seasoning his food. I have to wonder how many kids grow up thinking vegetables are disgusting because all they've been served are oversteamed flavorless and almost colorless piles of mush. One of his first words was *spice*, pronounced with two syllables, like a real little Texan.

Jackson's favorite breakfast is oatmeal. I make a big batch with thick-cut rolled oats, chia seeds, hemp seeds, raisins, cinnamon, and bananas every week, then freeze it in ice cube trays. In the mornings, I heat up three cubes of frozen oatmeal with one cube of frozen full-fat coconut milk. Sometimes I add blueberries, apples, leftover baked sweet potatoes, canned pumpkin, or shredded carrots. When he sees me putting his frozen cubes of breakfast in a bowl to be heated, he waves his hands in excitement and runs to his high chair begging me to put him in. He acts like the ninety seconds it takes to heat his breakfast is a lifetime. I feel a little bad that I've never made him pancakes or waffles, yet I figure, why change a good (and healthy) thing?

Sadly, as much as he loves his healthy legumes and grains, he'll coming running with equal delight and desperation when he hears that noise of a crinkling shiny wrapper. He can hear me open a Luna Bar from the front seat of the car and frantically throws his hand behind his head, reaching for me from his rear-facing car seat to share a bite with him. When I leave the pantry open, he sneaks in and comes out holding a bag of pretzels or baked snap peas in one hand, and with the other hand, he rubs his tummy in circles (his sign for "please"). How can I resist such a polite request?

BECKY

Our grandchild Anthony came to us this year via the miracle of adoption. Anthony is seven and into active guy stuff: sports and bikes and running and games, mostly activities he enjoys doing with his Poppy. He was over for lunch on a Sunday a few weeks ago, and we visited while I cleaned the kitchen and put together a take-home meal for his mom, who wasn't feeling well and had stayed home to rest.

"Hey, Anthony," I said, as I gave him a slice of orange, "would you like to help me cook sometime?"

"I love to cook!" he said as his beautiful brown eyes danced with excitement. Then he positioned the orange in his mouth so that the bright skin covered his teeth and asked me, in a muffled voice, to take his picture like that. I obliged and then picked up the conversation again. "Okay, Buddy, it's you and me in the kitchen sometime soon! We'll make something fun."

The kitchen is that happy place where both food and memories are made from scratch. From the little one dancing in the high chair to the six-year-old helping to roll out gingerbread men, to a teen flipping steaks on the outdoor grill—cooking together is universally loved by kids of all ages.

I'm currently reading the memoir, *Yes, Chef*, by Marcus Sammuelsson, who at age twenty-three was the youngest chef to ever be awarded three stars by the *New York Times*. He and his sister were adopted by loving Swedish parents as Ethiopian orphans. Marcus was two, his sister four. Some of his best memories are cooking in his grandmother's kitchen. "I never hesitate to give credit to (my grandmother) Helga who taught me not only how to cook, but how to appreciate food as a means to share experiences, stories and love," Marcus writes on his blog.

In his memoir, he shares how heartbroken he was when Helga, one of the people he loved most in this world, died. On the other hand, working in a kitchen with all those cooking fragrances about him every day made it easy to still feel connected to her. "The smell of chicken roasting, the smell of fresh herbs, the sound of onions sizzling in a pan would conjure up my grandmother and make her seem close."[6]

I hope that many years from now, even after I'm gone, my children and grandchildren will find comfort in their kitchens, that the smells of fresh-grated cheese, a hot skillet of cornbread, or savory roasted turkey will evoke memories of the fun we had together and the love I have for them that will last forever and always.

RECIPES KIDS LOVE TO EAT AND MAKE
Cinnamon Raisin Oatmeal

Jackson, now eighteen months old, happily eats this breakfast every day, and has done so for months. I make a batch each weekend, we all eat a bowl, and then I freeze the rest into ice cube trays for his weekday breakfast. —Rachel

Serves 4 adult-size portions (8 child portions).

- 3 cups of water
- 2 cups of milk of choice (I use organic unsweetened almond or coconut)
- ¼ teaspoon salt
- 2 cups thick-cut rolled oats (not quick-cooking)
- 2 tablespoons hemp seeds (optional, but if you leave out, reduce water by ¼ cup)
- 2 tablespoons chia seeds (optional, but if you leave out, reduce water by ¾ cup)
- 1 cup organic raisins or a diced or grated organic apple
- 1 teaspoon cinnamon
- 1 banana (very ripe mushy ones work best)

In a large sauce pan, bring water, milk, and salt to a low boil. Watch closely or you'll have a great big mess if it boils over. (Don't ask me how I know this.) Reduce heat to medium-low and add all the remaining ingredients. Cook on medium-low to low for about 10 minutes, stirring and mashing the banana occasionally, until the liquid is just absorbed. Serve immediately or freeze for later.

Freeze for later: Scoop oatmeal into ice trays and, with a spoon or spatula, spread it out evenly among the cubes, pressing down gently to make sure it's packed firmly. Cover tightly with plastic wrap and freeze. Once frozen, pop out and transfer to freezer bags. Reheat cubes in microwave with a splash of milk or a full-fat coconut milk. (I freeze leftovers when I don't finish a can.)

• Vegan/vegetarian
• Gluten free (use gluten-free oats)

Super Hero Green Smoothie

I made this smoothie for Jackson's first birthday morning. From his reaction, you'd have thought we bought him a new car. He applauded the blender as it pureed the greens and fruit into a delicious cold smoothie. (He delights in all things with a motor—vacuums, blow dryers, lawn mowers, anything that goes "vvvrooom.") And he let out an "ahhhh," after a big gulp from his sippy cup. —Rachel

Serves 2 (and a toddler).

3 tablespoons oats (optional)

1 tablespoon chia seeds plus 3 tablespoons warm water (optional)

1½ cups greens (I used a Power Greens mix of spinach, chard, and baby kale)

1 date, pitted

½ organic apple, seeded

1 clementine, peeled

1 banana, frozen or fresh

1 cup fresh or frozen pineapple

¼ teaspoon almond or vanilla extract

1 cup unsweetened coconut or almond milk

ice

Soak chia seeds in warm water, stirring occasionally until all the water is absorbed and the chia seeds are soft. Grind oats in blender into a fine dust. Turn off and add (in this order) chia seeds, greens, date, apple, clementine, banana, pineapple, almond or vanilla extract, and milk. Blend until smooth. Add a handful of ice if desired and blend again until smooth.

• Vegan/vegetarian
• Gluten free (use gluten-free oats)

90% Fruit Soft Serve

Why I didn't discover this simple trick to instant all-fruit ice cream years ago, I don't know. Last summer I made this several times a week for a refreshing dessert that I feel good about serving. It's fun to experiment with all kinds of fruit and combinations. —*Becky*

Serves 2–3.

1½ cups frozen fruit (such as black cherries, blueberries, strawberries, peaches, bananas, or a combination)

¼ cup of yogurt or almond milk or juice (really, any liquid you like)

1 teaspoon vanilla or any extract you desire (zest of lemon or lime or orange can also be used)

pinch of salt

2–4 tablespoons sugar or agave nectar or any other sweetener of your choice, to taste

any stir-ins you may like, such as chopped nuts, chocolate chips, coconut, peanut butter, and so on

Put all ingredients into a good food processor. Begin to pulse it, scraping as you go. Once the fruit is starting to pulverize, let the processor run several seconds as it works to turn the frozen fruit into a creamy texture. You will have to pause and scrape the sides of the food processor a few times and you may have to add a bit more liquid. Repeat this until you have a nice soft-serve fruit-based ice cream.

It takes a little patience. You can put the whole thing in the freezer for about 5 minutes to firm it up a bit more, or serve right away as is. Add any stir-ins you might want, or any toppings.

Suggested variations: bananas and chocolate syrup; bananas with rum flavoring and a stir-in of plumped raisins; pineapple with coconut milk; mango with orange juice; cherries with almond flavoring and chopped nuts; frozen apples with cinnamon; or kiwi and watermelon with green tea.

· Vegan/vegetarian (depending on mix-ins)
· Gluten free

Nate's Favorite Hairy Cheese Pizza

Though you could add a nice tomato sauce or other fancy toppings, this simple pizza, created by six-year-old Nate, is surprisingly tasty as is.
— Becky

Makes 1 pizza.

1 piece naan bread (I like Whole Food's garlic flavor)

1 tablespoon olive oil

½ cup finely grated cheese, preferably using a Microplane grater (Nate likes a sharp white cheddar cheese the best)

½ avocado, diced

any other toppings you like, such as turkey pepperoni, olives, or sundried tomatoes

Heat oil in a flat grill or pancake pan. Brown both sides of the naan bread until golden and crispy-crunchy. Cover with cheese and place in microwave or under broiler just until cheese melts. Dot with fresh avocado or any other toppings you like. Cut and serve.

· *Vegetarian (unless adding meat toppings)*

Chapter 11

Going Vegan in Cattle Country

When I was 88 years old, I gave up meat entirely and switched to a plant foods diet following a slight stroke. During the following months, I not only lost 50 pounds, but gained strength in my legs and picked up stamina. Now, at age 93, I'm on the same plant-based diet, and I still don't eat any meat or dairy products. I either swim, walk, or paddle a canoe daily and I feel the best I've felt since my heart problems began.

Dr. Benjamin Spock, world famous pediatrician
and author who lived to be ninety-six

RACHEL

So far, other than the few grandparent-given bites of cake and ice cream, Jackson eats what we eat, which makes him mostly a vegan baby. I am often asked if I will continue to raise him this way, and on one occasion I've been cursed at and called a terrible mother for depriving him of bacon and eggs.

Someday he'll be old enough to spend the night with friends and have class parties where cheesy pepperoni pizza will be the only thing to eat. One day, someone will poke fun at him for being vegan. I do want to shield him from feeling like the "weird kid," but more, I want to shield him from a future full of health problems and disease.

When Jared and I listened to the audio book about the benefits of a vegan lifestyle, which I mentioned in Chapter 3, I was already a bit of a health junky, having read a decent number of books on nutrition. The vegan way of eating seemed extreme. But without any other entertainment for the sixteen-hour road trip from Florida to Texas, we kept listening. When we crossed into Louisiana, we paused and chatted about all of these concepts that seemed to oppose everything we'd known about health. A particular study on the connection between casein, a protein found in milk, and cancer was both fascinating and flooring. *How could milk be bad for you?* we both wondered out loud. We'd been told for years it "does a body good." And as athletes, lean animal protein, and lots of it, had been an essential part of our healthy diets. But studies this book pointed to, like one done in China, were hard to ignore. In nonindustrial parts of China, where they consumed very little animal products, there were an incredibly low number of "diseases of affluence" (colon, lung, breast, leukemia, childhood brain, stomach, and liver cancers, as well as diabetes and coronary heart disease). The wealthier provinces were not healthier. In fact, the more industrialized (and thus wealthy enough to afford meat and dairy) a province was, the more prominent were these diseases of affluence.[7]

The information we listened to both infuriated and exhilarated me. I realized that with knowledge comes power, power to make a change, and I was intrigued enough to want to give a plant-based diet a try. I treaded lightly with Jared though, knowing there was no way my husband would ever consider giving up his steak and chili con queso. He ate almost nothing that grew from the ground or could be picked from a tree, which had been a real struggle for me. To my shock, Jared spoke up first.

"I feel duped," he said flatly.

"Me too," I nearly shouted, trying to temper my enthusiasm. "I've always considered myself very health conscious, but I feel like I fell for the Americanized version of what 'healthy eating' means."

"I think we should try a plant-based diet for a month," Jared proposed.

"What? Did you really just say you want to go *vegan*?" I sputtered.

"I don't want to be *a vegan*. I just want to try out this plant-based diet," he emphasized. Then, looking at my wide eyes, he added, "I know; I'm as shocked as you are."

After I addressed my concerns about his picky eating habits and he cleared me to cook whatever I wanted for the month, I gave it my all. "Okay, plant-based, vegan, whatever you want to call it is fine with me. Let's try it for thirty days and see how we feel."

We drove through a fast-food joint for our last good-old American meal. When we got home, our fridge was already empty from vacation, so we were able to start fresh. I dove into reading vegan food blogs and finding plant-based recipes to make. I was determined to give this new way of eating a valiant try, but leery about how long we could really last.

By the month's end, Jared felt better than ever. He had lost several pounds and had more energy. I, on the other hand, felt tired and irritable ... and hungry.

I wasn't sure I wanted to continue, but I saw my husband thriving and trying new vegetables and eating everything I cooked for him, even though he smothered most of it with that dang corn bean salsa. He wanted to keep going, so I decided to try one more month. My body must have been detoxing from twenty-six years of eating animals, because it wasn't an easy transition. But by the end of the second month, I finally seemed to adjust. I was learning how to nourish myself within new parameters of food choices. One revelation was that I simply needed to eat a greater volume of food than before. Restricting portions didn't work well, which was a rather nice surprise for someone who has relied on portion control as a way to stay trim. One of my mottos became "Every calorie must count toward nourishing my body." If I filled up on, say, tortilla chips, I was getting calories, but I was missing out on all the nutrients I could have given myself if I'd snacked, instead, on carrots and hummus.

A shift began to happen.

I started seeing my body as a gift to feed, to care for, to nourish … not to deprive. Every snack, meal, even dessert, was an opportunity to pour into my health and well-being. Oddly, cutting out all dairy, eggs, meat, and fish turned out to be the least restrictive diet I'd ever been on. I know that sounds unlikely, but with Jared's willingness to eat anything I cooked, no matter how weird it sounded, I was, for the first time, having a blast in the kitchen. Also, I've always struggled with the concept of moderation when it comes to food. Though I attempted it, I was never great at self-control and often ended up feeling guilty after a big meal or extra helping of dessert. Within the boundaries of a plant-based diet, however, I didn't have to restrict myself. I got to eat as much as I wanted and didn't gain weight. In fact, I lost weight and enjoyed the process.

An important note: I've used the words *plant-based* and *vegan* interchangeably, but they are not exactly the same thing. Technically, veganism is more than just a way of eating; it's a moral lifestyle that strives to live without all animal products. It's a lifestyle I admire and respect but not one I follow completely. And a plant-based diet is more than just eating like a vegan. A plant-based diet minimizes processed foods, sticking to whole grains, legumes, vegetables, fruit, nuts, and seeds. I strive to lean toward a plant-based diet, but in practice, I fall between the two categories. Labels are complicated.

We were living near Galveston, away from our family, at the time of our "conversion," and I remember our first family get-together after Jared and I became vegans. We were nervous. We hadn't told anyone, so Jared called his mom ahead of time to tell her we wouldn't be eating the tenderloin or the macaroni … or the green-bean casserole with bacon … or the rolls … or the cake. She seemed confused.

He put it out there as plainly as he could. "We're vegans now, Mom."

"What are *vegans*, exactly?" she asked.

I think she was afraid we had joined a wacky religious cult.

"It just means we don't eat meat, dairy, or eggs; it's an all plant-based diet," he said, then backpedaled in an attempt to soften the blow: "Rachel will make something for us to eat, so don't worry about us." He meant this to be reassuring, but to a mama's ears it must have sounded like her boy had just told her he was a Martian and would be eating green food from now on.

Easter dinner was awkward. As everyone piled their plates full of food, we dished out a serving of the Vegan Shepherd's Pie I made, which was literally the only thing we could eat. The fruit salad was dressed in Cool Whip (which actually has some real dairy in it, believe it or not). The green beans were cooked in bacon fat. The asparagus was cooked in butter. Even the salad had cheese sprinkled throughout.

Until that point, I really hadn't taken a great interest in cooking, nor had I been initiated into the tight circle of Women in the Kitchen. Nana and Rhonda were queens of that domain, and, honestly, until we changed our diets I had been happy with the arrangement. No one asked me to bring a pie or come early to help prep. I got to nap on Nana's couch with Jared after eating a big lunch someone else made for us. It was a pretty nice setup. Now I found myself in new and slightly strange territory. I was learning to cook, loving it, and suddenly found that I really wanted to be one of the Women in the Kitchen. If I could just get *in* I could speak up and say, "Hey, can I sauté a little of that asparagus separately in olive oil?" or "Would you mind if we left the cheese on the side of the salad?"

As my confidence grew in the kitchen, and as the Randolphs realized these "vegan shenanigans" might actually be sticking around, I eventually navigated my place among the Women in the Kitchen. I learned to speak up. It was an adjustment ... for all of us. When we didn't eat the beans simmered with bacon, we had to explain that we couldn't just "eat around the bacon," and had to clarify that vegetable soup cooked in chicken stock was not vegan.

I haven't asked for anyone to eat differently on our behalf, and I never request that they leave out the bacon. I do ask what I can bring, though. I ask what is being served and make a dish that is filling enough for a main dish but also complements the rest of the meal as a side for the omnivores among us. Or sometimes I just host the meal myself.

This year we had Easter lunch at our house. I cooked a beautiful vegan feast of zucchini risotto, macaroni and cashew cheese, roasted vegetables, massaged kale, and three-pea salad. Rhonda brought a roast. We came together at one table, not as vegans or omnivores, but as a family bonded by love. After lunch, I woke Jackson from his nap and dressed him in his Easter outfit, baby-blue plaid pants and white-collared shirt with a sweater vest over the top. I grabbed the white newsboy hat off the wall, where it had been hanging since my baby shower, and placed it on his sweet head. Tears filled Rhonda's eyes as we returned to the kitchen and she saw her grandson donning the hat her own son had worn as a baby. Jackson looked adorable as he hunted for Easter eggs, like an old man on the golf course searching for his ball.

When I'm not hosting, bless their hearts, Rhonda and Nana have learned to make a few adjustments, purely out of love. Nana keeps vegan butter in the fridge now and uses it in the dishes she cooks for us. Instead of smoked ham, Rhonda recently made a delicious Crock-Pot of barbecue beans, simmered in a smoky barbecue sauce. She's also learned what we like at a nearby Chinese restaurant and brings that to us for dinner on occasion. These little acts of kindness and thoughtfulness go a long way in making us feel loved, respected, and valued at the family table.

With so many people these days going vegan, vegetarian, gluten free, or dairy free, learning a few tricks or recipes to make them feel welcome and included can be an act of love and respect.

You may not agree with their reasons or understand an allergy. You may find it frustrating or inconvenient. You may even find yourself feeling emotionally upset or sorrowful over the change. You've always shown your child or spouse how much you love them with their favorite meal or special treat, and suddenly they won't eat it anymore. It feels like rejection. You used to meet your best friend for a beer and hot wings, and now they want to meet over sake and edamame. Change is hard. Even small changes.

Jared always got a big box of cheese crackers for Christmas next to his stocking. And when it was my special day, my mom made me my favorite Strawberry Pretzel Jell-O dessert. (Alas, loaded with cream cheese and whipping cream.) When Christmases and birthdays came along, our families struggled with how to show their love for us. Our moms no longer knew our favorite indulgence. It's a hard pill to swallow when you feel like you no longer know "the way to your child's heart" or you have to say goodbye to a food-based tradition that you've always shared with a loved one.

My mom tried to make a vegan version of the pretzel Jell-O dish. It wasn't the same. We discovered that there are just some foods, like cream cheese and certain meats, for which there is no equal or tasty substitute—especially when they are the main star of a dish. There was a season of transition, of finding our way into creating new food memories. I commend both of our families. Instead of being bitter or clinging to those feelings of rejection, they chose to find new ways to love us.

My mom, who enjoys variety and new opportunities, saw our diet as a new and fun culinary challenge, a chance to get even more creative with cooking and to add even more variety to her recipe arsenal. When I visit, she cooks a vegan feast. And I do mean *feast*. On more than one occasion she has tried to sneak frozen blocks of leftovers into my carry-on luggage. "If soup is frozen, it is no longer liquid," she assured me. "Surely the TSA paid enough attention in chemistry to know *that*."

Each trip, I try to explain to Mom that I appreciate her cooking but that I can't possibly eat four casseroles, two batches of cookies, and two pies, *on top* of the three meals a day she prepared for my four-day visit. When we went vegan, it was like she became the classic Jewish mother, trying to stuff us with lots of food, to make sure we had all the nutrients we needed and would never go hungry. I finally had to tell her, gently, "I remember telling you that we eat a greater volume of food as vegans, and I know you've really taken that to heart. But that just means we might want an extra serving of lentils, not an extra gallon of them."

We are celebrating the end of this book with a trip to Denver for the holidays. Mom sent me a list of vegan dishes she plans to prepare while we are there, and though I know they will all be delicious, we may have to invite every vegan in Denver to join us to eat through the list.

BECKY

People ask me if I worry about Jared and Rachel and the baby not eating milk or meat or eggs. To be honest, I might be concerned if it were anybody but Rachel. And I was a little concerned at first. Actually, I never dreamed they'd stick with a strict vegan diet! We all knew that Jared loved his grilled and barbecued meats, and cheesy nachos. At the time he made the decision to go vegan, he ate almost no vegetables, so we all wondered, "What will Jared eat? He will starve!" Rachel has always loved a wide variety of vegetables and fruits. Going vegan was a challenge for both of them, but for Jared especially, this was a *radical* change from his former way of eating. That he and Rachel have eaten vegan for three years and continue to love the vegan lifestyle, has amazed everyone and truly impressed me.

As you know by now, my daughter is one smart cookie, a good researcher, and knows more about nutrition than almost anyone I know. She and Jared look amazing, feel great, and Jackson is the picture of health and strength. These days, I honestly don't worry about them. I admire them. I know Rachel will make dietary adjustments if needed in the future, but for now who can argue with success?

I actually enjoy the challenge of cooking vegan when Rachel is visiting, and I often prefer the dishes I make for her and Jared to the ones I've made for us carnivores. When I do eat mostly plant-based foods, with a little animal protein thrown in (more as a garnish, the way it is used in Asian countries), my stomach feels flatter, and my digestion is almost instantly better. Whenever I start feeling heavy or bloated, I will have a vegan day and feel lots better. Gradually, and in large part because of Rachel's influence and tasty recipes, I've come to prefer plant-based meals. If given a choice between a juicy hamburger or a marinated portobello-mushroom sandwich with grilled red peppers, eggplant slices, and onions—I am going to go with the portobello hands down every time.

Still, I live with and cook for lots of meat eaters. Hospitality is a way of life for us. If I were to become a strict vegan or vegetarian, it would be tough to serve meals to clients and guests and friends. We travel a lot in places where you cannot always find a great vegetarian or vegan meal. So I do not see us adopting a strictly plant-based diet.

That said, however, I am all for incorporating more vegetarian and vegan meals into our diet and serving more creative veggies in general to our family and guests. I am experimenting and learning, stretching and trying. One of my goals is to continue adding more plant-based foods into our diet and trim back the amount of meat we eat.

Many dishes can be easily tweaked for special diets. When Rachel and Jared come, I often do buffet type meals: Asian rice bowls with edamame and tofu along with chicken or shrimp; or warmed tortillas that can be filled with all sorts of Mexican fare from ground beef to beans. A salad or pasta bar is also easy to set up, and lots of soups can be simmered in vegetable broth (to my surprise, I like the taste of vegetable broth better than chicken or beef) with a dish of cheese or meat served on the side. Everyone can create what they want, and it's no big deal for me to cook and serve this way.

I never mind cooking for those with special dietary needs. I always ask about allergies these days when we have new guests over for a meal. And almost always, someone is allergic to something or following a special food plan for their health. I enjoy having lots of beautiful and delicious food on a table for guests on all sorts of diets. It makes them feel valued, which they are. For me, it is a form of kindness and love and serving, just one more way of giving a cup of cold water in Jesus's name.

RACHEL

"Will you stay vegan forever?"

"Will we raise Jackson vegan?"

Two questions people often ask.

The answer is, "I don't know."

Though I admit I've gained a soft spot for lovable livestock in the last couple of years too, and the idea of eating animals no longer appeals to me, we went vegan mostly for our health. As long as Jackson continues to grow well while eating a balanced plant-based diet, I don't see why we'd change. I'm open to adjusting how we eat if I ever feel that his health (or ours) is anything but thriving. Right now he is the model of a healthy, happy boy — strong and energetic, above average on the growth charts.

Research shows that people who eat a plant-based diet have much lower rates of heart disease, cholesterol, diabetes, arthritis, and cancer. I've lost some close friends in my life to tragic accidents — things that no one except a recluse can avoid. I'd be crazy to think I can shield my family from *all* the bad things that could happen to them. But if there's a chance, even just a small chance, that I can shield us from cancer or a heart attack, I think I'd be crazy not to try. I want Jackson to be healthy, and I want him to have two healthy parents that will be around to nag him to get a job and find a nice girl to settle down with. I want to play with his children someday ... and his children's children. When your life is happy and good and you feel well, you really want it to be a long one.

I love this quote from the documentary *Forks Over Knives*, comparing the extremity of a plant-based diet to coronary bypass surgery: "Some people say that eating a plant-based diet is extreme. But millions of people this year will have their bodies cut open, and a vein from their leg sewed onto their heart.... Some might also say that's extreme."[8]

My grandfather on my mom's side of the family just had a heart attack and a stint put in to open an artery. Granny has always been health-conscious, but she emailed me as soon as they returned from the hospital, asking me if I could send her some of my best vegan recipes. She wants to give her beloved husband the best possible chance at recovery, a healthy heart, and a long life. I called her back and excitedly shared some encouraging studies with her about heart disease patients who have switched to a plant-based diet. Like Dr. Esselstyn's study of twenty-three patients with severe heart disease (many had basically been sent home to die). Five dropped out in the first two years, leaving eighteen participants. Eleven years into the study, there was only one minor coronary event (and that was from a participant who had strayed from the diet). These were very sick patients. In the decade prior to the study, collectively they had suffered forty-nine separate coronary events. The decade following: one.[9]

My Granny was as fascinated as I was when I had first read

this study. She asked if she could borrow a few books from my library. I'm happily packing up my copies of *The China Study, Prevent and Reverse Heart Disease* (C. Esselstyn), and *The Engine 2 Diet* (R. Esselstyn)[10] this weekend to send to her. Though I'm not an evangelist or even an expert on plant-based diets, when someone is eager to learn more about this lifestyle we live, I'm always thrilled to share everything I've learned in the past few years.

Mom has incorporated lots of vegan meals and dishes into her diet because, yes, they are healthy, but even more, she tells me she likes them better! She and Greg both prefer vegan mac 'n' cheese (made with cashews), and Mom is so crazy about a vegan sausage, made from Field Roast with sage and apple, I recommended that she prefers it and uses it exclusively now. She makes two kinds of vegan chili that people liked just as well, or even better, than her meat-based recipe in a side by side taste test at a recent big party. She tries to have one or two vegan days a week and always feels better those days.

Eating vegan has given me a true passion for cooking. It isn't hardship. It's fun. It doesn't feel extreme. We cook more than we eat out. We pack our lunches. I've started carrying an avocado in my purse, which I'll often add to a salad or sandwich at restaurants with limited vegan options. I carry a bottle of almond milk with me when I go to work at a coffee shop so I don't have to pay extra for their soy milk. These things are just part of my routine now.

I have memories of my Granny pulling out a bottle of stevia from her purse, years before stevia was popular, to sweeten her tea. (She swears it has kept her from catching colds as a side benefit.) Little things like this seem no stranger to me than carrying around a pack of gum or a protein bar.

I've prayerfully sought God's guidance with each step of our health journey, and that is how I will continue. There will always be people who don't like or understand the decisions I make, whether we stay vegan or not, and that's okay. I don't feed my family like this to make a statement or to save the planet. I do it out of love. I do it because I want to have many, many years of wellness to enjoy gathering together at the table or around the kitchen counter with my family.

When Vegans Come to Dinner

Mom and I thought it would be helpful to share a few tips we've learned when it comes to cooking for the "weird" eater in your family. A lot of recipes you already know and love are either vegan or can easily be made that way if you learn a few simple tricks to replace some common ingredients.

Eggs

If you have a recipe for a baked good, like muffins or bread, that calls for an egg or two, you can use a flax egg (combine 1 tablespoon flax meal with 3 tablespoons of warm water and let it sit for 5 minutes before adding to the batter). One half a banana or a half cup of applesauce will also work in a sweet dish. You can also find Ener-G Egg Replacer at most grocery stores.

Dairy

Butter: Earth Balance margarine can be used in place of butter in most baked goods. Vegetable shortening can be used in things like vegan icing. Use coconut oil or olive oil for sautéing.

Milk: Almond milk, coconut milk (in cartons, not the canned variety), soy milk (organic preferably), and rice milk are all readily available dairy-free milks. I use organic unsweetened almond milk for drinking and in most of my recipes. Because of soy milk's high protein content, it tends to have the best results in baked goods. You can even add a teaspoon of vinegar or lemon juice to a cup to make a soy buttermilk for baking. I give coconut milk to Jackson to drink because of its high healthy fats. Rice milk offers very little nutrition, but has the mildest flavor.

Cheese: Vegan cheese substitutes are getting better all the time. Daiya is the most common shredded cheese substitute. Be careful for "lactose-free" cheeses, because those typically contain casein, a milk protein. My favorite cheeses have been the ones I've made from nuts and nutritional yeast, like a cashew-based mac and cheese sauce, or a cashew queso dip. There are also great recipes online for cheeses like ricotta or Parmesan. Mostly I've just weaned myself from cheese, though. Despite what most of us have been led to believe, not everything needs to be topped, smothered, or sprinkled with cheese. Good flavorful food doesn't need it. If you need a good greasy cheese fix though (as an occasional treat), most Whole Foods stores will make a pizza with Daiya cheese for no extra charge, and many pizza places will let you bring in your own cheese.

What about cream? Believe it or not, vegans can have their cake, their ice cream, and their whipped cream too. You can easily find vegan cream cheese and sour creams in stores now. And we've discovered a whipped cream that rivals the "real deal." A can of full-fat coconut separates when chilled. If you whip the thick cream that floats to the top with a touch of sugar and vanilla, it makes a fluffy and decadent whipped topping. Mom is a real whipped cream snob and this has become her go-to whipped topping. It's really that good.

Protein: You may not want to assume that the vegans in your life will be thrilled with nothing but a fake chicken breast as their main entree. Some people love these fake meat products, but many of us, especially the ones who try to follow a plant-based diet, don't actually eat many processed fake products. I have found a few meat substitutes that I really like. Field Roast Applewood Sausages are my favorite. They are GMO-free (that is, free of genetically modified organisms) and soy-free and taste delicious and are omnivore approved. Whole Foods has a Chick'n Salad in their deli that is quite good. It does use processed fake chicken, so I just have it for an occasional treat. I use tofu about once a week and tempeh and seiten on occasion. But really, you don't need to use fake meat or even soy to feed a vegan. Lentils, split-peas, chickpeas, and beans are all healthy filling options and can easily replace the meat in a lot of recipes. And believe it or not, grains and veggies almost all pack protein as well.

DAIRY-, EGG-, AND MEAT-FREE RECIPES THE WHOLE FAMILY WILL LOVE
Cashew Queso

My omnivore friends beg me to bring this to all of our parties. I pinky-promise you, it looks and tastes just like real cheese dip, but it's seriously guilt free. Every ingredient is good for you. Bake your own chips and you've got yourself a truly indulgent tasting, yet completely healthy plate of nachos! —*Rachel*

Makes 3 cups.

- 1¼ cups raw, unsalted cashews (roasted, unsalted work too if you can't find raw ones)
- 2 tablespoons nutritional yeast (available at Whole Foods or health food stores)
- 2 tablespoons onion powder
- 1½ teaspoons salt
- ½ roasted orange or red bell pepper* (I've also used a small jar of pimentos)
- 2 cups water
- 1 teaspoon lemon juice

---

* You can buy roasted peppers in a jar, but making your own is easy. Just place a whole bell pepper directly on a gas burner flame, rotating them a few times with heat-proof tongs, or place them on a pan under the broiler until the skin gets charred and black in several spots. Then put them in a bowl tightly covered with plastic wrap for about 5 minutes. Rub off most of the skin with a damp paper towel. Voila, roasted peppers!

In a food processor, blend cashews, nutritional yeast, salt, and onion powder into a fine dust. Add about ½ cup of the water and the roasted bell pepper and blend again. Pulse in the rest of the water and lemon juice. Transfer mixture to a pot and heat on medium heat, stirring often until it has thickened to the consistency you like. Keep warm in a small Crock-Pot for entertaining, stirring every so often. If it gets too thick, just stir in a little more water.

- Vegan/vegetarian
- Gluten free

No-Bake Apricot Bars

If I had to pick a favorite recipe, it would be this one. It was inspired by one of my favorite vegan food bloggers, Angela Liddon's recipe for "5 Ingredient No Bake Vegan Date Squares" (www.ohsheglows.com). I've since made several variations, and they've become a family staple among my mom, Granny, and Aunt Rachel. They are filling enough for breakfast, sweet enough for dessert, and healthy enough for a guilt-free anytime snack. Just make them. You won't regret it. —Rachel

Serves 12.

Crust

1½ cups whole cashews (toasted, roasted, honey roasted—whatever you have)

1½ cups regular or thick-cut oats (not quick-cooking)

½ teaspoon kosher salt (omit if cashews are salted)

10–15 dried apricots (about half a cup), roughly chopped

¼ cup coconut oil, melted

Filling

25–35 dried apricots roughly chopped (2 cups)

½–1 cup water

Crust: Spray a muffin tin (my preference) or an 8x8 pan with nonstick cooking spray. In a food processor, process cashews, salt, and oats until a fine crumble forms. Add apricots and process until crumbly again. Add coconut oil and process until sticky. Remove from processor. Set aside ¾ cup of the mixture for later. Press remaining mixture into cupcake molds or pan to form a crust. For muffin tins, put a heaping tablespoon into each mold; then use the back of the spoon to press down and smooth out the layer.

Filling: Process the apricots and ½ cup water in the food processor (I've found a smaller bowl works better than a large one if you have a full-sized food processor — in fact, I just use my mini one for this step) until a paste forms, stopping to scrape down the sides and adding a little more water as needed (don't exceed 1 cup). Scoop out the apricot mixture into the pan or evenly into the muffin tins and gently spread out to cover the crust.

Sprinkle on the reserved crust and gently press down into the apricot mixture, just so it sticks. Freeze for at least an hour or until firm. Cut squares or pop out of muffin molds and wrap individually with plastic wrap. Store in freezer. Enjoy straight from the freezer or slightly thawed as a delicious healthy treat!

Variations: Try it with dates and almonds or dried cranberries and pecans or dried cherries and walnuts.

- Vegan/vegetarian
- Gluten-free friendly (use gluten-free oats)

Roasted Red Pepper Quinoa

Quinoa (pronounced KEEN-wah) has the highest protein content of all grains and is a complete protein. I like to have it on hand for quick dinners because it cooks in about 20 minutes (compared to 45 for whole-grain rice). It's similar to couscous, but much better for you. This is my go-to recipe. It would be perfect with the tofu version of my mom's Blackened Tilapia recipe in Chapter 2 and some steamed broccoli. — Rachel

Serves 4.

  ½ cup onion, diced

  2 garlic cloves, minced

  1 tablespoon olive oil

  1 cup quinoa (rinsed if the package doesn't say it's pre-rinsed)

  1½ cups of water

  ½ cup of juice from a jar of roasted red peppers
    (or ½ cup more water)

  ½ teaspoon salt

  ½ cup roasted red peppers, chopped (I use jarred peppers for this
    recipe because I like to use the juice too, but you can roast
    your own [see Cashew Queso recipe for instructions] and use
    all water instead)

In a skillet or sauce pan, sauté onions in the olive oil until soft, add
the garlic and sauté a few minutes longer.

With a Rice Maker: Transfer the onions and garlic and any
remaining oil into the rice maker; add the quinoa, water, salt, and
red pepper juice. Stir, cover, and start the rice maker. (If your rice
maker has a tendency to stick, add about a teaspoon of extra oil
before stirring.) When the rice maker goes off, add in the chopped
roasted red peppers.

Without a Rice Maker: Add the quinoa, water, red pepper
juice, and salt to the sauce pan. Cover, bring to a boil, then reduce
to simmer, and cook until all the liquid is absorbed (about 15 to
20 minutes). Stir in the chopped roasted red peppers.

· Vegan/vegetarian
· Gluten free

Sweet Potato Lentil Chili

*I have a spicy version of this chili on our blog, but I made this milder,
sweeter version for myself when the baby was coming. If you like spice,
though, feel free to use more peppers or cayenne. This makes a lot, so*

you can freeze leftovers and have a vegan, gluten-free, nut-free, and soy-free meal on hand if a guest with allergies pops in for dinner.
—Rachel

Makes about 3 quarts.

- 3 tablespoons olive oil
- 1 onion, diced
- 3 carrots, chopped
- 1 celery rib, chopped
- ½ cup sweet red, yellow, or orange peppers (for spicy version use a poblano instead or add a jalapeño or serrano pepper to the mix)
- 3 garlic cloves, minced
- 1 teaspoon grated fresh ginger (if you have it)
- 1 teaspoon salt
- 1 tablespoon cumin
- 1 tablespoon chili powder
- ½ teaspoon cayenne (optional)
- 1 chipotle in adobo sauce, chopped fine (or 1 teaspoon chipotle powder or 2 teaspoons extra chili powder)
- 1 sweet potato, chopped
- 1 28-ounce can of diced fire-roasted tomatoes
- 1 15-ounce can of sweet potato puree (pumpkin or butternut squash work too)
- 1½ cups dry green lentils, sorted for dirt and rocks* and rinsed
- 8 cups water
- 2 cups of frozen corn, thawed
- 2 cups kale, removed from stem
- *Other:* brown rice, quinoa, or crackers to serve with

---

* Before cooking any dried legumes, pour them onto a few paper towels and sort through them looking for sticks, little rocks, or clumps of dirt. Please don't skip this step. I find something in probably half my dried beans. You don't want you or your guests to bite into a rock!

In a large pot, heat olive oil and sauté onions, carrots, celery, peppers, garlic, and ginger with 1 teaspoon salt on medium heat until veggies are soft. Stir in cumin, chili powder, cayenne, and the chipotle. Add chopped sweet potato, tomatoes, sweet-potato puree, lentils, and water. Cover and bring to a boil. Lower to a simmer for 30 minutes with the lid tilted, stirring occasionally. Remove the lid. Add corn and kale (if freezing, don't add kale yet). Bring back to a boil and then lower to simmer for another 10 minutes or until you reach the desired consistency.

Serve over brown rice, quinoa, or with crackers.

- Vegan/vegetarian
- Gluten free

Chapter 12

Tangible Love in a Casserole

*There is communion of more than our bodies
when bread is broken and wine drunk.*

M. F. K. Fisher

BECKY

A few weeks after Christmas, in the wee morning hours, I woke to shouts coming from downstairs. Nothing like hollering at 3:00 a.m. to bring one quickly to consciousness. I was out of bed in a flash.

"Are you okay?" I yelled down the stairs.

"No!" Greg's voice moaned. "I'm not! I need your help!"

I found my husband doubled up in excruciating pain on the bottom step in too much agony to move a muscle. We quickly agreed this was a situation for paramedics; there was no way he could walk nor could I get him to the car.

I am normally scatterbrained and prone to anxiety, but in life-or-death emergencies I get eerily calm, focused, and controlled. I once remained calm and collected as I gave a choking woman the Heimlich maneuver (she thanked me for saving her life after expelling the chunk of pineapple lodged in her throat); but my knees go weak and I can run from the room, nauseous and shaky, if someone gets a bad paper cut. Thankfully, in this moment I was all calm and focus.

I met the ambulance at the hospital, and it didn't take long to determine Greg had a kidney stone. People always describe their kidney stone experience, ending with "It was even worse than childbirth." Having given birth to four children in natural, cozy, excruciating pain, I was doubtful. But I am no longer a skeptic. My husband was suffering, equal to any woman in transition.

I don't know how many doses of pain medication the nurses had to give Greg to finally numb his agony, but I do know it was enough to turn my very practical, clear-headed husband into a hippie stoner. He went from writhing in pain to examining his hands as if they were marvelous works of art he had never noticed before. At one point he looked at me, glassy-eyed, and smiled. "I've always liked the way shampoo looks when it runs through my hands in the shower."

I smiled and patted his legs, which were sticking out from his pastel hospital gown. "Well, isn't that special?"

Two days and several downloads of Dilaudid later, the doctor confirmed that the "stone was stuck in the sword" and would need to be surgically removed. We texted our pastor, Hugh Halter, who is also Greg's best buddy, and asked him to say a prayer for the operation. Like the sensitive man of God he is, Hugh texted back, "I will certainly pray. But, hey, if the Big Guy doesn't make it, ask him if I can have his golf clubs." We laughed, even though it hurt Greg a lot to do so. I kissed the love of my life as he was wheeled away, then grinned like a madwoman to keep from crying. As soon as he was out of sight, I looked for a secluded spot in the waiting room where I could sit and pray and worry, all by my lonesome.

Before I could form a single alarming thought, however, my friend Michele walked around the corner, seemingly from out of nowhere, and hugged me. In one hand she held my favorite Starbucks drink and in another a box of her huge, world-famous, homemade chocolate chip cookies. This was no easy feat because Michele and her husband had recently taken in three very young children in need of a safe haven. Two of the little angels trailed behind her, carrying a get-well card. Michele had no way of knowing chocolate chip cookies were Greg's Number 2 weakness and attraction. (I would, of course, be Number 1.) Her calm, cheerful presence distracted me from what surely would have been thirty minutes of contemplating Worst Case Scenarios, all of them ending with me as a sobbing widow, explaining how my husband died from a kidney stone.

Mercifully, the doctor appeared, announcing the super-fast surgery a complete success, though a lingering fever would keep Greg in the hospital for an additional night. Greg had not been able to eat anything for hours before the surgery, so even the pale, frail-looking hospital meal tasted good to him. When I showed him the box of Michele's super-sized chocolaty, buttery homemade cookies and passed them back and forth under his nose, he closed his eyes and smiled. He was deeply touched by Michele's thoughtfulness and said so, as he munched through two giant cookies with a glass of milk, in record time. Then he lay back on his pillow at peace, out of pain, tummy happy, and thoroughly pampered. I smiled at him lying there, eyes closed, sighing happily, looking so much like a little boy — with a bit of cookie crumb on his cheek and a milk moustache, on his real moustache. Food, made with love and delivered in times of human vulnerability, may be the ultimate manna for the body and soul.

～

One of my best friends, Lindsey, and I share a private joke: "I'll bring meatloaf."

It all began when a major problem of overwhelming proportions dropped into her lap one day, and, on my way out the door to meet her at a restaurant for a crisis management discussion, I looked in my fridge and grabbed what I had on hand — some leftover meatloaf. Others might have stopped to pick up flowers or a card or perhaps a book to encourage their hurting friend. Leave it to me to grab leftover meatloaf. Someone is hurting? My auto-response is to feed them. When people are in pain, I turn into a character not unlike the mothers from *My Big Fat Greek Wedding*. "You no feel happy? No worry, I make you meatloaf."

I listened empathically as my good friend shared her heart-wrenching dilemma, hopefully creating a soft, safe space for her pain to land. As we parted, I reached down to my bag and pulled out a Tupperware container.

"I'm so sorry you are going through this. With all my heart, I wish I could fix everything. But since I can't, I brought meatloaf."

We both laughed, even through the misty tears. And that's how "meatloaf" became a symbol of tangible caring between us. As in most friendships, Lindsey and I have taken turns being in crisis, so it wasn't long before something tough happened in my life, and I was the one in emotional agony. This time my friend brought me the "meatloaf"—which evolved to mean comfort food in any form: from a bottle of wine to a home-cooked meal to guacamole and chips at a favorite Mexican joint. After a recent minor surgery, she showed up at the door with a feast to put any Greek mother to shame: marinated grilled chicken on pita bread, accompanied by homemade tzatziki and a mint-feta-watermelon salad. Forget the pain pills; this food had healing powers. With every bite, I felt physically, emotionally, and spiritually nourished in body and soul, for such is the power of a meal prepared with love.

Recently a friend who was walking through a painful crisis came to stay the night, have supper, and enjoy some much needed TLC. She and I visited over wine as I chopped, grilled, and roasted. Out of the mess that was now my kitchen came a beautiful spread: fresh Norwegian salmon, topped with a salsa of peaches and avocados with a little lime, salt, and sugar, surrounded by roasted mushrooms, sweet peppers, and summer squash. To the side sat Lindsey's famous Greek watermelon salad.

My friend surveyed both the damage and the outcome and said, "Becky, just standing in your kitchen is healing to me."

I didn't know whether to laugh or cry. The kitchen has become a place for nurturing souls as well as coaxing good meals into being. Cooking also serves as a living metaphor, for beauty and delight does not appear in a vacuum of a perfectly ordered and clean life, or kitchen. It takes a lot of messes, small and large, to create a life—and a feast—worth its weight in goodness.

~

My friend Julie and I had known each other since our teens. We bonded through church camps, boy-dramas, and fresh faith experienced during the hippie-like days of the Jesus Movement.

Julie passed away this last year after a brave battle against a brain tumor, and I'm still struggling to believe she's gone. Though the tumor certainly took its toll on her body for over two years, I have to say that this tumor never took her joy. Julie was the happiest, most positive, and most grateful cancer patient I've ever seen. She spent these last years traveling and reconnecting with dozens of friends and family members she had known and loved over the course of her full and giving life.

Two years ago, near the beginning of her diagnosis, after her brain surgery, I flew to California to be with Julie for a week. She was staying in a two-bedroom hotel suite near the cancer hospital. (Not only did Julie have a tumor, but she was also going through a horrific divorce after thirty years of marriage.) I soon realized that my love of naps, the slow and quiet pace to my days, and my joy in cooking made me the perfect companion for a convalescing patient. When I arrived, there was little in the way of fresh food in Julie's hotel pantry and fridge. Because of her inability to do much on her own at this point, the kitchen was stocked with premade meals that could be microwaved easily. As I surveyed the goods, I couldn't help noticing a gallon-sized jar of beautiful olives sitting on the counter.

"I've got a thing about olives. They were a gift from my aunt," Julie said with a smile.

"Then I know just the meal I want to whip up for you." Thankfully, Julie's appetite was coming back in full force that week. I made a quick run to Trader Joe's, filling my cart with all things fresh, colorful, and flavorful, then made myself at home in the tiny kitchen, throwing together a fragrant briny-sweet sauce of olives, garlic, tomatoes, and artichokes, which I served over beautiful lemon-pepper ribbons of pasta. The puttanesca sauce that Rachel and I had created together seemed perfect for this meal. We sat down to eat at the little hotel dining table, the late summer sun casting warm beams through the window on the one-bowl-meal before us. Julie took my hand and offered a heartfelt prayer of thanksgiving and then took a bite of the pasta dish, practically humming with delight as she ate. Then she looked up at me, tears glistening, and said, "Becky, I don't think I've ever been happier than I am right now."

"Julie, you've got to be kidding!" I said with a laugh.

"No, I mean it," she said. "I've had a series of kind friends and family stay with me these past few weeks, and you are like the cherry on top of the sundae of love I've been showered with. And this meal tastes better than anything I've had in months. My cancer has given me clarity. Trust me, good food, good friends, a peaceful place, God with us—these are the best things in life."

Like a good Southern-raised girl, I "aw-shucks-ed" and downplayed the simplicity of what I'd done, emphasizing Julie's strong positive spirit and deep faith, but even as I protested I could see in her eyes that she was, indeed, serenely, deeply, gloriously happy. I'm not saying a good home-cooked meal can chase away the horrors of cancer. But I am saying that a simple dinner prepared with love for someone who is dear to your heart, has a power beyond the food itself.

"Take, eat, remember," Jesus said as he served his friends bread and wine that last night before he died. In addition to the symbolism of flesh and blood, I see something else exemplified. Jesus could have chosen from a hundred ways to say goodbye, yet he carefully chose the setting: a table, friends, bread, wine. He must have known there is a human connection between food and memory. So when grandmothers and mothers throughout the centuries say to their children and grandchildren, "Take! Eat! Enjoy!" those kids will savor and remember the taste of food mingled with love —perhaps that is also holy; perhaps that too is a sacrament.

The summer of 2012 was a tough one for our home state of Colorado. First, wildfires came down from the forest into Colorado Springs communities, destroying many homes and interrupting thousands of lives with uncertainty and fear. Then came the morning we woke up to the news of random shooting violence in a theater just twenty minutes from our home. Every person has different reactions to personal and community tragedy. Oddly enough, mine was to cry, pray, and then tie on an apron. In light of pain that is too large or random to grasp with my mind, I am often overwhelmed by the urge to cook something comforting, stabilizing, and warm.

Like tears—cooking, serving, and eating together is a language without words that hearts understand.

"I cook my little omelet in the pan for the glory of God," said Brother Lawrence, a seventeenth-century monk (and cook) who wrote *The Practice of the Presence of God*. What if every time we tied an apron around us or flicked on the stovetop flame, we said a prayer and cooked our little meals for the glory of God? And as we are cooking for others, what if we prayed that our food would bless their bodies, and in some mysterious way, also bless their souls? We can nourish our loved ones in intangible ways as we feed them tangibly.

A few months ago I picked up a little hand-embroidered pillow at an estate sale. It says, "Hospitality is a form of worship." I have to admit, I came to this realization late in life. I wish I'd been more the domestic kitchen-lovin' woman back when my kids were younger. I was so busy with four teens, an oft-difficult first marriage, and an intense and time-consuming writing and speaking career that good home-cooked meals were embarrassingly rare. I could so easily get melancholy about the past—so much I would do differently if I could do it all over again—but regrets do not help. I am here now. My kids are all adults, but they still come home—and often!—to my happy kitchen, bringing their little ones with them, and though I know that I came late to the cooking party, I have finally arrived with heartfelt enthusiasm.

I had a great mentor in my own mother. Warmth and love poured from Ruthie's kitchen, with the comforting sounds of coffee percolating as background music. With all the ways she nourished bodies and souls, in fact, I could fill a Rolodex with "Mom and Food Memories."

I see her pouring a steaming cup of coffee, to be served alongside thick slices of homemade coconut cake (in those days before she nixed sugar), accompanied by conversation with some hurting soul at our kitchen table.

I watched the weekly ritual of my mother, dressed in her high heels, Sunday dress, and apron, popping a roast in the oven—big enough to serve surprise company after church.

I would sometimes accompany her as she carried a casserole to someone who just had a baby or lost a loved one, and I would marvel at the natural ease with which she knew exactly what to say or do to cheer or comfort.

What I learned from my mother was that I had the power to

ease pain and bring joy to others simply by using the tools lying around my kitchen. Then, when I was in my early thirties, my mother showed me how to soothe and cheer others by putting into words the funny or inspiring stories lying around in my head.

The older I get, the more I think the main purpose of life is to offer healing and blessing to whoever God drops in our path with whatever he's given you. For us, that often means shared laughter over life's craziness, a soft shoulder to cry on, or a hot meal prepared with love. My daughter and I come from a long line of women who laugh, cry, and cook. (And then fight over who gets to write about it; though we usually concede the material to the relative with the closest deadline.)

We're women who, armed with skillets and laptops and a penchant for comforting chick-chat, do our small part to lighten the world's burdens, one kitchen table moment at a time.

> Food, like a loving touch or a glimpse of divine power,
> has that ability to comfort.
> Norman Kolpas

"BRINGING THE MEATLOAF" – RECIPES THAT SHOW TANGIBLE LOVE IN A CASSEROLE
Lindsey O'Connor's Refreshing Watermelon, Mint, and Feta Salad

This is one of my absolute favorite summer side dishes. —*Becky*

Serves 4.

Salad

    4 cups of cold, cubed watermelon (cut in 1-inch squares)

    1 cup cubed or crumbled feta (if dicing, make them about ½-inch square)

    ¼ cup finely minced mint leaves

Vinaigrette

   a piece of watermelon to equal about ¼ cup

   1 teaspoon honey

   1 tablespoon lime juice

   ¼ cup extra-virgin olive oil (*Becky's note:* dressing may be served
      without the addition of oil if you prefer it lighter)

Place watermelon, feta, and mint in large salad bowl. Blend ingredients for vinaigrette together in blender; gently toss with other ingredients and serve.

   • *Vegetarian*
   • *Vegan (omit feta)*
   • *Gluten free*

Momma's Sweet 'n' Spicy Meatloaves

This meatloaf will cure anything from hunger to heartache. You'll never need or want another meatloaf recipe after you try this one.
— Becky

Serves 6 to 10.

Meatloaf

   1 package of dry Lipton onion soup mix

   2 slices of soft wheat bread

   2 eggs

   ¼ cup water

   ⅓ cup catsup

   2 pounds ground lean beef or bison (preferably organic,
      grass-fed, no antibiotics)

Sauce

   ⅔ cup catsup

   ⅓ cup bottled chunky-style salsa

   ⅓ cup brown sugar

Put the first five ingredients in a blender or food processor and blend. Pour this mixture into a big bowl along with 2 pounds of ground beef (or bison). Using your hands (I put little disposable sandwich bags on as "gloves"), work the seasoning-bread mixture into the beef. Pat into a 9x13 casserole dish. Using the side of your hand or end of a wooden spoon, "cut" the flat loaf into equal "mini loaves." It will look like little irrigation ditches alongside the mounds of meat. Bake 20–30 minutes or until loaves are cooked through, draining off any grease as the meatloaves bake — once about halfway through cooking, and once more when the meatloaves are done.

While meat is cooking, make the sauce: put catsup, brown sugar, and salsa in sauce pan; heat and stir until sugar melts. When meatloaves are done, ladle the sauce over the top. (If you have some left over, save it and serve with the meal for those who want extra.) Put loaves-with-sauce back in oven and turn to broil. Broil until sauce is thickened and caramelized.

· *Gluten free (use gluten-free bread)*

Michele Cushatt's Famous Chocolate Chip Cookies

I hope you treat this recipe like the gold it is, because Michele's chocolate chip cookies are hands down the best I've ever eaten. Such a treat for her to share them with all of us. — Becky

Makes about 4 dozen regular-size cookies, but Michele makes them bigger-than-average-in size, to yield about 3 dozen.

1 stick (½ cup) real butter, softened
½ cup butter-flavored Crisco
1 teaspoon vanilla
2 eggs
¾ cup brown sugar

¾ cup sugar
2¼ cups flour
1 teaspoon salt
1 teaspoon baking soda
12 ounces Ghirardelli or Nestlé chocolate chips

Preheat oven to 350°. Put butter, shortening, vanilla, eggs, and both sugars in a mixing bowl and cream on medium speed until light. Add flour, salt, and soda and mix until blended. Stir in chocolate chips. Drop by spoonfuls onto cookie sheet and bake for 12 minutes or until golden brown. Then deliver to your favorite people.

· *Vegetarian*

Orange Glazed Carrots

Sometimes it is the simplest things that elevate a lowly veggie. Butter, brown sugar, and orange juice work magic on carrots. —Becky

Makes four ½-cup servings.

2 cups diced or mini carrots
1 tablespoon water
½ cup orange juice
¼ cup brown sugar
1 tablespoon butter
sea salt to taste

Put the carrots and a tablespoon of water in a tightly covered microwave-proof dish and nuke for about 12 minutes or until just tender. (You can also steam them if you prefer.) While the carrots are cooking, put orange juice, brown sugar, and butter into a pan on the stovetop. Turn burner on high until it reaches a boil; then turn down to a simmer and simmer for about 6 minutes or until the mixture reduces and starts to get syrupy. Add the cooked carrots to the orange syrup and simmer 1–2 minutes more until carrots are coated with thick buttery syrup and taste like heaven. Sprinkle with a little sea salt and serve.

· *Vegetarian*
· *Vegan (use vegan margarine, i.e., Earth Balance)*
· *Gluten free*

Acknowledgments

So many talented, loving, giving people helped bring this book into being.

Greg Johnson not only makes an amazing husband and step-dad, but as our literary agent, he was the first to tell us he thought we'd make a great mother-daughter writing team. From the moment Greg heard the title and concept and saw sample chapters, he was 100 percent behind us, pitching the proposal with enthusiasm and tasting the recipes with even more excitement. We love and appreciate you, Greg, for all that you do behind the scenes so that we can simply focus on writing.

On a personal note, Becky would like to thank Greg for being the sort of husband every woman dreams of marrying: loving, positive, supportive, kind, romantic, patient, and fun. A gentle leader, whose shoulder I can always lean on. Without you, my love, where would I be?

Thank you to Jared, from Rachel, for believing in me and loving me relentlessly. You are the most kind and patient man I've ever met. (And as you know, I'm an expert in administering patience tests, so I'm a credible judge in such matters.) Thank you for giving your weekends and evenings to help with Jackson while I write and cook, and for your willingness to try all my recipes, even the weird ones. You forever have my heart. (Becky would like to add that Jared is an answer to her prayers. No one could ask for a better son-in-law or father to her grandson.)

Carolyn McCready, you are not only one of the most delight-ful friends and kindest people we've ever met, but a true dream editor. We are tremendously grateful for your talents in shaping and focusing, and guiding and encouraging our words. It is a much better book because of your brilliant input. All that plus you attended a food bloggers conference with us with baby Jackson in tow and introduced us to the fabulous, funky town of Portland. The fun morning we spent at Powell's bookstore, including coffee and a pastry-to-die-for and browsing shelf after shelf of food writing, was a memory to cherish (and hopefully repeat). Thank you for championing us at every turn. We love you!

Special thanks to Tom Dean, another longtime friend, fabulous all-around guy, and the best marketing pro we could have asked for, and to his publicity sidekick, Katie Beth, for working so hard to promote this book. Bob Hudson and Sarah Kuipers, thank you for bringing your fine editorial skills to this manuscript. We are so blessed to have landed with Zondervan and such a topnotch team of professionals and goodhearted people.

We must thank Ruthie Arnold, Becky's mother and Rachel's "Granny," who taught all her girls to laugh, write, cook, and pray —pretty much all the skills needed for a meaningful and happy life. Your and Daddy's constant faith in a God who is loving and kind taught us to look up with trust in the worst of times and give grateful praise in the best of times.

Rhonda Randolph is Rachel's mother-in-law and a fun-loving energetic Mimi. Thank you so much, Rhonda, for giving Rachel breaks to write as you cared for Jackson. Knowing he was so happy with you and his Pop gave peace of mind to both of us. And while we're at it, thank you for raising such a fine son as Jared.

Thank you to Rachel St. John-Gilbert, Becky's sister and Rachel's namesake and aunt. Not only are you a wonderful, witty author who understands the writing life; you are that perfect blend of a friend: funny, empathic, and encouraging. Thank you for helping babysit one active baby Jackson now and again during the writing of this book and letting him give you a head-to-toe workout. We owe you a glass of wine and bottle of Advil.

A shout-out to Gabe, Becky's youngest son, Rachel's brother, who has been especially encouraging during the writing of this book; and in his shared love of food, entertaining, and cooking together.

Becky would like to give hugs to Anthony, Nate, George, Titus, and Jackson, who have made being a "Nonny" ridiculously fun. You give me stories to remember and laugh over and cherish every time I'm with you. I love you, my adorable grandsons, to the moon and back! (And your Auntie Rachel loves her four nephews too!)

Rachel has some special words for her son, Jackson Ray: You were just a newborn when we started this book and my journey as a mother began. Oh, how you have filled our home with joy and laughter! You have changed my life in every way for the better. I love you, my sweet boy.

Rachel can't forget Jackson's Mother's Day Out teachers. Ms. Rhonda, Ms. Heidi, and Ms. Michalla, you were answers to this anxious momma's prayers. Thank you for giving me peace of mind and giving Jackson a safe and loving place to learn, grow, and explore while I wrote.

Thank you also to girlfriends who added to the stories in this book and to the stories of our lives, who prayed for and cheered us along the way: special thanks to Michelle Rusch, Lindsey O'Connor, Michele Cushatt, Lucille Zimmerman, Patricia Raybon, Melissa Gantt, and the ladies in Rachel's MOPS group.

Notes

1. Paula Butturini, *Keeping the Feast: One Couple's Story of Love, Food, and Healing* (New York: Riverhead Books, 2011), 6.

2. Nigel Slater, *Toast: The Story of a Boy's Hunger* (London: Gotham, 2011), 1.

3. Carol Lynn Pearson, *I'll Always Be Your Daughter: A Fable for Mothers and Daughters* (Layton, Utah: Gibbs Smith, 2010).

4. Shauna Niequist, *Cold Tangerines* (Grand Rapids: Zondervan, 2007), 229.

5. Lucille Zimmerman, *Renewed: Finding Your Inner Happy in an Overwhelmed World* (Nashville: Abingdon, 2013), 6.

6. Marcus Sammuelsson, *Yes, Chef: A Memoir* (New York: Random House, 2012), 206.

7. T. Colin Campbell and Thomas M. Campbell, *The China Study: The Most Comprehensive Study of Nutrition Ever Conducted and the Startling Implications for Diet, Weight Loss, and Long-Term Health* (Dallas: BenBella, 2006).

8. Lee Fulkerson, director, *Forks Over Knives* DVD (Virgil Films and Entertainment: 2011).

9. Campbell and Campbell, *The China Study*.

10. Caldwell B. Esselstyn Jr., *Prevent and Reverse Heart Disease: The Revolutionary, Scientifically Proven, Nutrition-Based Cure* (New York: Avery Trade, 2008); and Rip Esselstyn, *The Engine 2 Diet: The Texas Firefighter's 28-Day Save-Your-Life Plan That Lowers Cholesterol and Burns Away the Pounds* (New York: Grand Central Life & Style, 2009).

Indexes

Recipes by Category

veg — Vegetarian
V — Vegan
gf — Gluten free

(see "Recipe Notation Glossary on page 11 for definitions)

Note: Any required substitutions or modifications are listed at the end of the recipe.

The Main Attractions

One Bowl Wonders (Soups, Stews, and Chilis)

Fresh Corn and Roasted Poblano Chowder *(veg/V/gf)*, 88

Stewed Summer Veggies *(veg/V/gf)*, 137

Sweet Potato Lentil Chili *(veg/V/gf)*, 194

Tortilla Soup *(veg/V/gf)*, 157

Yellow Pepper Soup *(veg/V/gf)*, 120

Show-Stealing Sides

Broccoli Carrot Slaw *(veg/V/gf)*, 139

Lindsey O'Connor's Refreshing Watermelon, Mint & Feta salad
(veg/V/gf), 205

Orange Glazed Carrots *(veg/V/gf)*, 208

Oven-Blistered Potatoes *(veg/V/gf)*, 138

Roasted Red Pepper Quinoa *(veg/V/gf)*, 193

Party Pleasers (Appetizers and Snacks)

"Carrot Cake" Chutney & Cream Cheese Topping for Nana's
Beloved Crackers *(veg/V/gf)*, 102

Cashew Queso *(veg/V/gf)*, 191

Jared's 15-Alarm (and 3-Fire-Truck) Roasted Corn Bean Salsa
(veg/V/gf), 54

Killer Chipotle and Roasted Pepper Salsa *(veg/V/gf)*, 56

Warm Stuffed Dates *(veg/V/gf)*, 44

White Bean Guacamole *(veg/V/gf)*, 55

Morning Munchies

Cinnamon Raisin Oatmeal *(veg/V/gf)*, 172

Sweet Potato Pecan Pie Oatmeal Bake *(veg/V/gf)*, 86

Sweet Treats

Happy Sips

Recipes by Chapter

CHAPTER 1: *Favorite Family Recipes*

CHAPTER 2: *Foolproof Recipes for the Distracted Home Cook*

Becky and Rachel would love you to drop by for a visit at their food blog, where they regularly share new recipes with pictures and stories that keep them inspired in the kitchen.

www.laughcrycook.com

Share Your Thoughts

With the Author: Your comments will be forwarded to the author when you send them to *zauthor@zondervan.com*.

With Zondervan: Submit your review of this book by writing to *zreview@zondervan.com*.

Free Online Resources at

www.zondervan.com

Daily Bible Verses and Devotions: Enrich your life with daily Bible verses or devotions that help you start every morning focused on God. Visit www.zondervan.com/newsletters.

Free Email Publications: Sign up for newsletters on Christian living, academic resources, church ministry, fiction, children's resources, and more. Visit www.zondervan.com/newsletters.

Zondervan Bible Search: Find and compare Bible passages in a variety of translations at www.zondervanbiblesearch.com.

Other Benefits: Register to receive online benefits like coupons and special offers, or to participate in research.